Knox Bhavan

craft material detail

Knox Bhavan

Artifice
books on architecture

I tell you, it is easier to build a grand opera or a city centre than to build a personal house.

— **Alvar Aalto**

Contents

Ted Cullinan

We call architecture the more or less subtle but deliberate composition of places, large or small: region or city, down to dwellings and the component bits of dwellings. We used to learn the 'Art of Architecture' from looking and by practising and working for other architects.

Today, we learn by more or less the same process and by attending architecture school. Sometimes architecture school encourages us to fly before we can walk: either to design whole cities (or worlds) or to draw abstractions on a smaller scale, but in either case to design them to be constructed out of material X. If pressed, a designer might say of material X, "Oh it's concrete", or "Oh it's steel", or "Oh it's plastic", or "Oh it's glass", and so on. So the general form is composed or designed, but its detailed construction (out of stuff) has no effect on the form, or the form on the detailed construction (out of stuff).

Of course, we do live in a technological world in which it is quite possible to design general form and only decide late in the day how to make it or what to make it of. But how could the form of Le Corbusier's Chapel at Ronchamp have been conceived except by imagining it to have been made of concrete on mesh? And how could the Hopkins Olympic Velodrome have been imagined other than in laminated timber, used to contain the exact dimensions required by cycle racing and watching?

And, in the same way, consider Sasha Bhavan's and Simon Knox's Rigg Beck house in the Lake District of England. Here, the use of local Westmorland stone in various forms is as essential an element in the design of the house as is its overall form; or better to say the materials and the form both contain the essence of one another.

The overall three-dimensional form of the house consists of a long gallery for living in, broken only by an upper-level entrance; below this long gallery another long gallery for sleeping in, the bedrooms individually curved out towards the beck. Study, main bedroom, sitting room and a bottom-level games room make ends as special places for both galleries.

"Simon Knox and Sasha Bhavan are as skilful in the design and making of furniture as they are in the material making of buildings."

— **Ted Cullinan**

Is it not wonderful to be able to describe it thus, so simply, without the usual "Here is the front door, here is the wall, the door on the left leads to the living room, the door on the right to the dining kitchen, the stair up to the bedrooms is in front of you and the cloakroom is down the hall", etc, as is necessary in a more usual contemporary 'knotted up' house plan? Rather than this, one can go straight from this general formal description to discuss how it is celebrated in the manner and detail of its building: and I think this is true of all the Knox Bhavan schemes illustrated in this lovely book.

The lower ground and ground floor walls are masonry cavity walls whose outer layer is dry-laid Westmorland slate that is tilted to drain outwards, and the windows in these walls are of oak, framed by dressed Lazonby stone—the ends curve as is typical of dry stone walling, and all of this heaviness enhances the 'bottomness' of the bottom of the form of the building.

On the upper floor, the outer walls are from Westmorland slate, being lighter and having more openings; and lighter still are the lower floor sawn-timber bows of the bedrooms. The whole is crowned by a vaulted ceiling below a roof finished with recycled Westmorland roofing slates laid properly in diminishing courses. The quality of light coming into the building is both suitable to its parts and lovely as a whole, as a glance at the picture of the downstairs gallery will confirm.

And that leads me to the furniture. Just as one feels one can predict the building details by knowing the overall form, so you feel you can predict the quality and grace of the interior and exterior furnishings and fittings by knowing how it's built. Suffice it to say that Simon Knox and Sasha Bhavan are as skilful in the design and making of furniture as they are in the material making of buildings, as they are in the larger form of them.

"... one can go straight from general formal description [of the house] to discuss how it is celebrated in the manner and detail of its building: and I think this is true of all the Knox Bhavan schemes illustrated in this lovely book."

— **Ted Cullinan**

This book has been laid out in nine chapters using individual buildings to describe different aspects of composition through matter. This has left me free to use one building of theirs to illustrate what I feel concerning their overall achievement.

I wish there were many other architects like them.

Ted Cullinan is an inquisitive inventor and passionate composer and maker of buildings. He is an inspiring, eminent and internationally renowned teacher. In 2008 he was awarded the Royal Gold Medal in recognition of his substantial contribution to international architecture.

"It is a really generous thing to build a building well", says Sasha Bhavan. She is thinking of the long hours builders are putting in to get the glazed surface to Knox Bhavan's new office pond just right, the glazed brick above the waterline, the brick slips below.

She is also thinking of happy sunny lunchtimes and snatched moments when she, Simon Knox and the team will be able to look at those bricks with pride unclouded by a sigh at what might have been, if only the care had been taken to line them up. The carp too will be happy; the writhing family of colour which you step over to enter Knox Bhavan's current Peckham office of 15 years will be transplanted.

It is perhaps hard to recognise such qualities until you are a client yourself, but Knox Bhavan's buildings and way of practice encompass that spirit of generosity. To work with Knox Bhavan is to be enfolded in the warmth of artistry and craft that distinguishes their buildings. It is to be drawn in—as client, contractor, subcontractor or consultant—to an understanding of how genuinely good buildings can be created. And that, it turns out, is not only by thoughtful and demanding design, but also by drawing out the best in all those working on it. Unlike in many practices, here the Polish builders step out of the shadows and turn into stonemason stars deeply invested in perfecting the building. The unexpected hero of multi-award winning house Holly Barn is the contractor who declares he can easily build to the nearest half brick—hardly a reassurance of accuracy—then proceeds to take this Norfolk Broads home to joinery-level detail. The clients, who wanted an open, manoeuvrable home with rooms for when the family descended without the staleness of shut-off bedrooms, have their own reward in Crowbrook House.

How do Knox Bhavan get to work with these amazing people? They make them amazing. Recognising what people are good at is a rare gift. Encouraging them to apply that with pride is even rarer. Not only this, but it is cultivated by Knox Bhavan; they want to take people through things, step by step, they understand the importance of the handover party including those who make, but rarely see, the finished building. The client of one home, giving out pewter tankards to the whole team who had worked on it, demonstrates how these values are imbued across the project.

"Recognising what people are good at is a rare gift. Encouraging them to apply that with pride is even rarer.... [Knox Bhavan] want to take people through things, step by step, they understand the importance of the handover party including those who make, but rarely see, the finished building."

— Eleanor Young

Not that there is much chummy clinking of tankards during a project. The practice is exacting: if the apex of a roof joint is to be invisible, rooflights have to be detailed to keep it so. If a veneer is being selected the veneerers might not expect to include the sap, but if Knox Bhavan have decided to keep it then it is for a good reason. There are detailed questions to be asked and understood, as clients make informed decisions as collaborators. This is in return for Knox Bhavan concerning themselves with the everyday journey through other people's lives, so at the 19 holiday homes at Camber Sands they know exactly where the wetsuits will be peeled off. At Russell Square Cafe in central London they instinctively feel how people will come rushing in for a coffee, then want to sit contemplating the grand square through their windows.

This is a practice that grew out of an expressive and humanist tradition most clearly seen in the work of Edward (Ted) Cullinan, who introduces this book. Here worked the three architects who made Knox Bhavan what it is: Sasha Bhavan, Simon Knox and Mary-Lou Arscott. It was a time in the practice and the lives of those there that turned it into a family, building the Cullinan's office together in Islington, growing up together. Jeremy Till, educator, polemicist and head of Central St Martins, has picked up on this strand of sustainable and social architecture that works for people as getting on with the "important issues of social empowerment through better (social) space".

And so we see the tradition tempered by a more linear modernism in Penoyre & Prasad Architects (where Simon Knox worked even before Cullinan's) and by Knox Bhavan who apply their expertise at the most human level to homes, cafes, offices, education spaces and, importantly, to the social spaces around those buildings. In architecture and planning, context is oft talked about but not always understood. Of course a new building changes the very context it goes into, but it can make the most of it, complete it or even open up future possibilities. The London Brownstones in Dulwich attest to this, the pair of handsome stone houses filling the missing tooth in the smile of an Edwardian terrace. At Rigg Beck, the rugged stone of the house reads as an extension of the landscape around it, a topographical spur. It appears to be at one with its surroundings in a way that much modern architecture is not, borrowing the organic relationship that can seem solely the preserve of rural vernacular from times past.

"The expressive tradition is enriched by Knox Bhavan's deep understanding of materials, as close to a craftsman's as you see among architects."

— **Eleanor Young**

The expressive tradition is enriched by Knox Bhavan's deep understanding of materials, as close to a craftsman's as you see among architects. The hard apprenticeship in materials came for Simon as he took on a painstakingly perfectable project for a member of the Sainsbury family at The Little Boltons in Chelsea, as Knox Bhavan was founded. Running the job effectively as a contractor as well as designing on site, alongside the makers, resulted in beautiful pieces of timber joinery and handles, things that mark out many of the practice's projects over the years and have been recognised by the rigorous Wood Awards that look for timber and architectural excellence. And the practice's first major foray in aluminium won them the Aluminium Imagination Award for the 1,200 m^2 office and residential Tudor House in Guernsey. A test cast still sits happily in their office, appropriated as a bike holder. It is no coincidence that the practice has chosen to focus on materials in this book.

The care, however, doesn't stop at the elemental materials of metal, stone and timber. Knox Bhavan ask more from the building blocks of architecture, of wall, door, window, ceiling. Each one has to perform its part to make the building right and to make them so much more than they might be in other hands. Walls are not determinedly rectilinear but allowed, where right, to flow. Ceilings are attended to and an unexpected, yet delightful, sensation in a Knox Bhavan building is of a heavy load being lifted from your brows as the ceiling curves up or light is reflected in from above to illuminate a bathroom deep within a plan. For these, among other things, the practice has been acknowledged with nine RIBA Awards including the RIBA's Manser Medal for House of the Year in 2006, a remarkable result when set against the number of projects Knox Bhavan have completed.

"The care however, doesn't stop at the elemental materials of metal, stone and timber. Knox Bhavan ask more from the building blocks of architecture, of wall, door, window, ceiling. Each one has to perform its part to make the building right and to make them so much more than they might be in other hands."

— **Eleanor Young**

For 20 years, with a small team, Simon and Sasha have been crafting and completing beautiful and unusual buildings. Embedded in their Peckham base, they have made Dulwich and South London a far richer place by applying their understanding of space and inhabitation while revelling in the opportunities of different settings beyond their locale. The next chapter in the practice's development has been signalled by the design of a new office, minutes away from the practice's historic base, and Simon and Sasha's long-cherished plans to design themselves a home now coming close to fruition. This book is another step forward, a consolidation of what the practice has done so far, a reflection on the foundation that Knox Bhavan has built up over the years and the skills and dedication that takes. I am torn between lobbying to visit their next remarkable home for a client and wanting to see those generous skills applied to other building types: the lessons of designing gloriously non-institutional homes for the infirm and wheelchair-bound taken into healthcare; the essence of inhabitation into education. I hope we shall see all of these.

And in case that sounds all a bit serious—it isn't. My favourite detail comes from the Knox Bhavan toilet, a deep, but tiny, basin handily snuck in alongside cistern casing that makes the smallest room work. Source: caravan. Verdict: ingenious.

Eleanor Young writes about architecture, place and people. She is executive editor at the RIBA Journal.

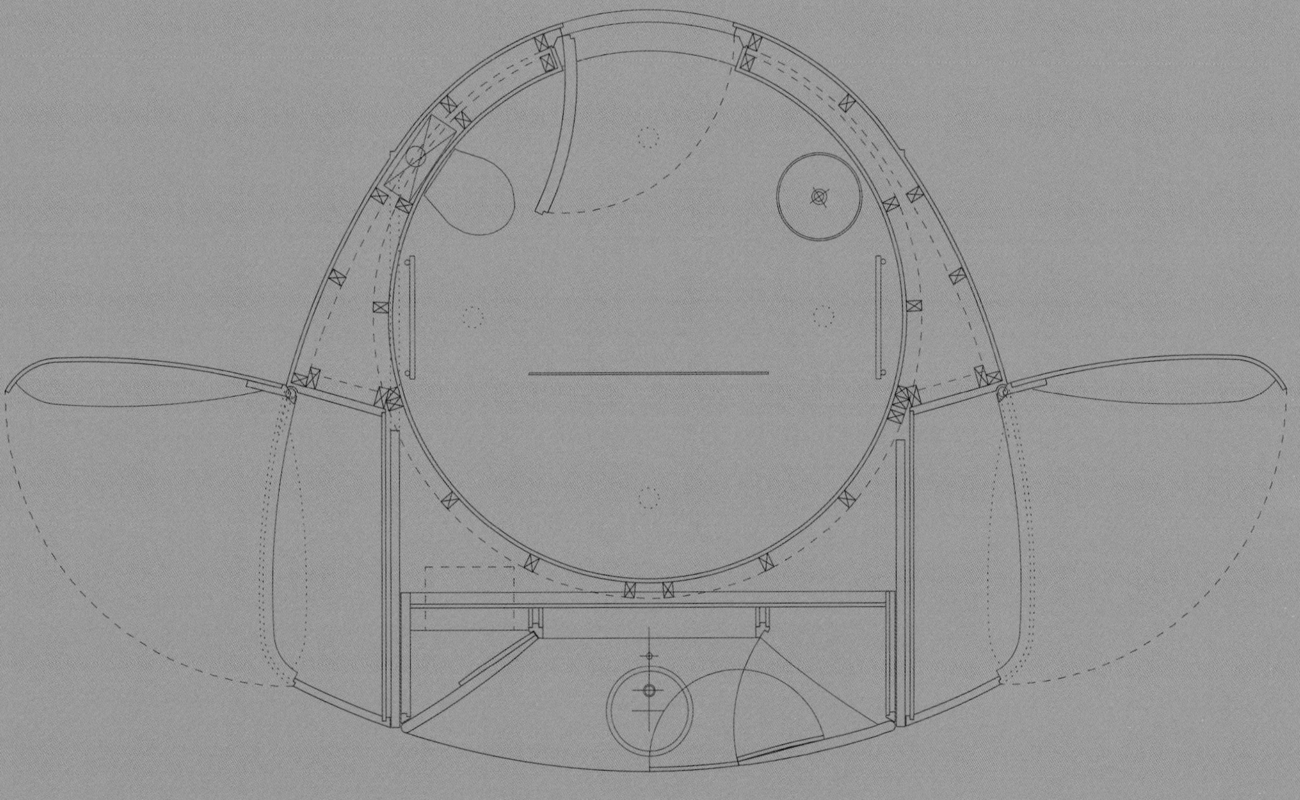

Chapter one

Growing and Developing
New Maltings
Suffolk, 2003

Growing and Developing

The building programme at New Maltings can be measured in decades. Originally designed by gold-medal winning Ted Cullinan in the 1960s for the Knox family (no relation), a second phase of buried lower ground floor bedrooms was added by Mark Beedle (then in the Cullinan office) in the 1970s. This was followed by a third phase of work involving major remodelling in the late 1980s by Sunand Prasad and Simon Knox at the newly formed practice Penoyre & Prasad. In the late 1990s Sunand passed an enquiry for a fourth phase of work to us. This was for a new pavilion that became one of our first realised new-build projects in 2003. So a number of architects over the decades have contributed to the overall scheme and each have gone on to hand the project over to a younger emerging practice, and all remain friends. The history of this project, therefore, makes it particularly unique and special for us.

Ted's original 'Knox House' was long and thin with interconnecting family rooms positioned on the south side looking out across the Stour Valley. The brief our client gave us was to add a completely independent pavilion, with flexibility. It was to provide 'his and her' studies, doubling up as extra bedrooms when needed. A shower, toilet and small kitchen would make the pavilion self-contained. The brief clearly stipulated that the new pavilion had to relate harmoniously to the existing house, and be made from complementary, and if appropriate, matching materials.

There was space to build this pavilion between the existing house, and a 3 m high beech hedge on the eastern site boundary. The new pavilion is the same width (6 m) as the original 1960s house. It is constructed from the same palette of materials: local stock brick, western red cedar boarding, large aluminium windows and a long strip copper roof with a generous south-facing overhang.

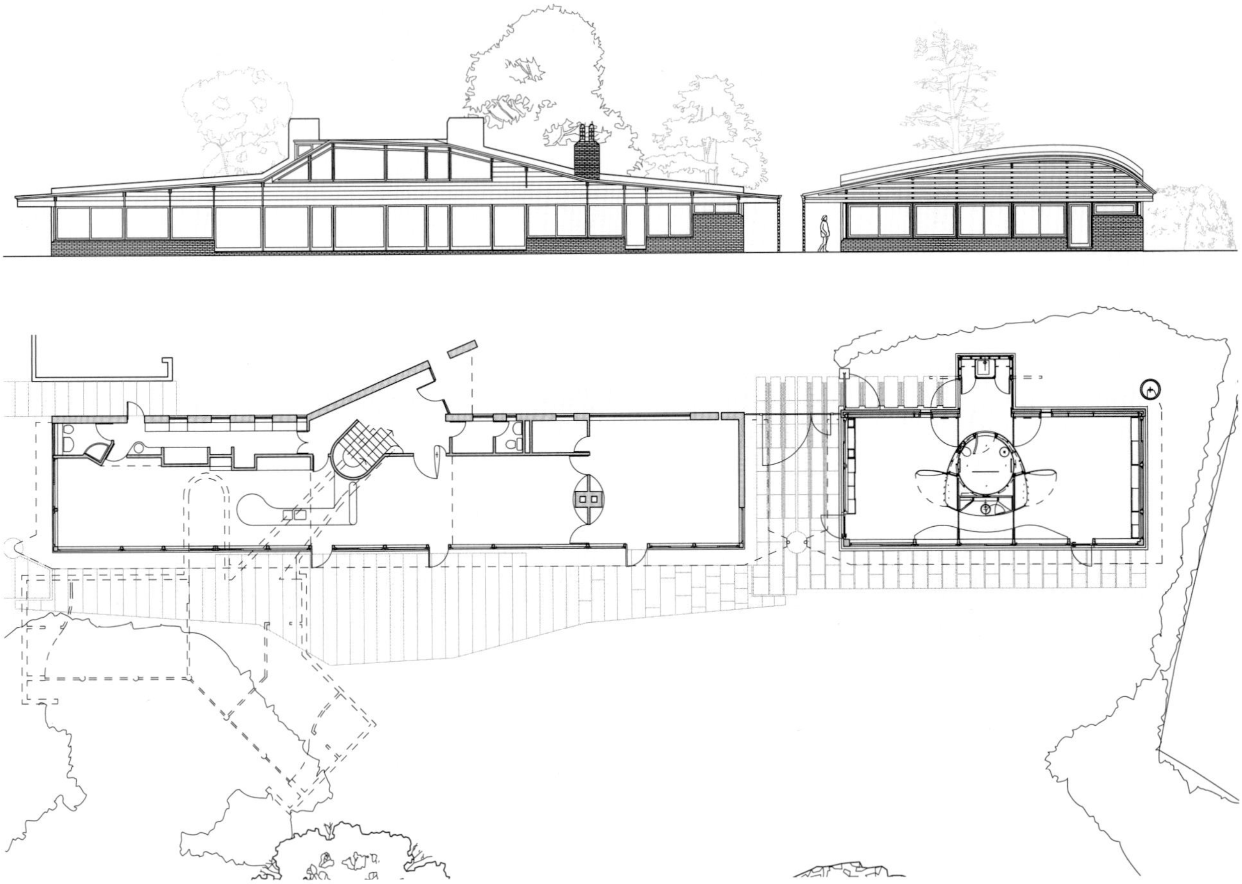

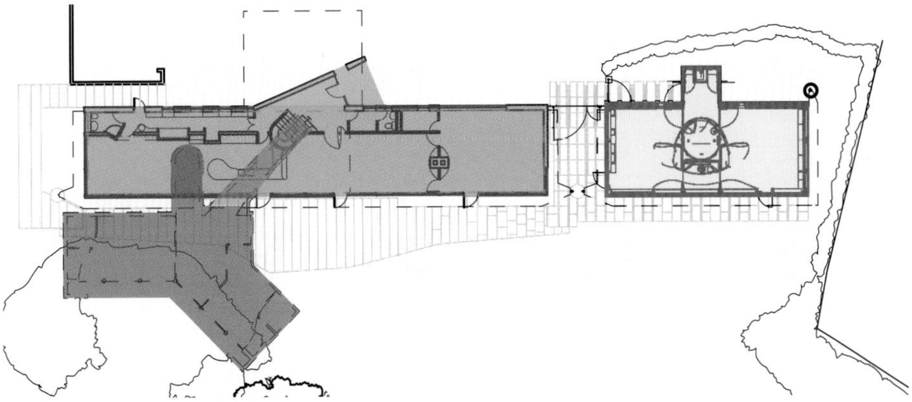

The original
Ted Cullinan 'Knox House'
1960s

The first extension
underterrace bedroom
1970s

The second extension
new porch
1980s

The new pavilion
2000s

opposite left
construction photos—forming the curves in plan and section.

opposite right
original Ted Cullinan's 'Knox House'.

top elevation and plan—new pavilion and original 'Knox House'.

bottom plan—colour coded.

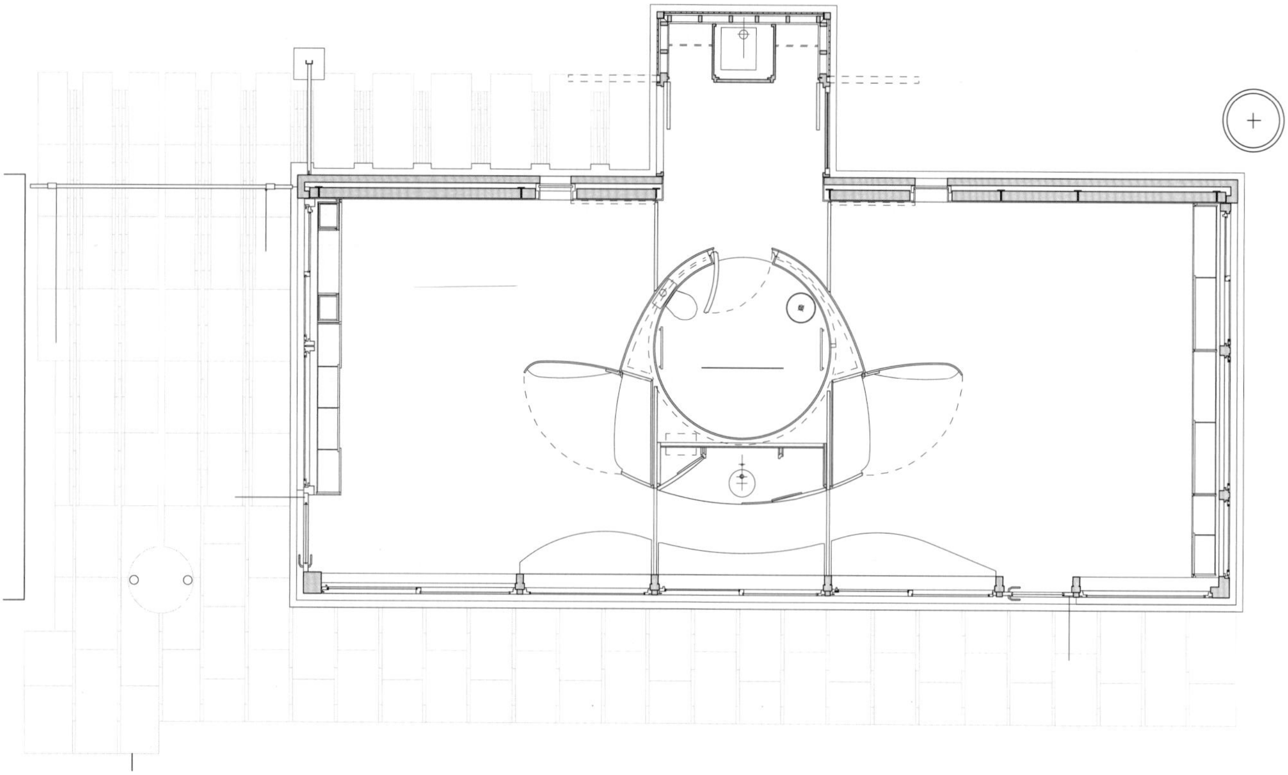

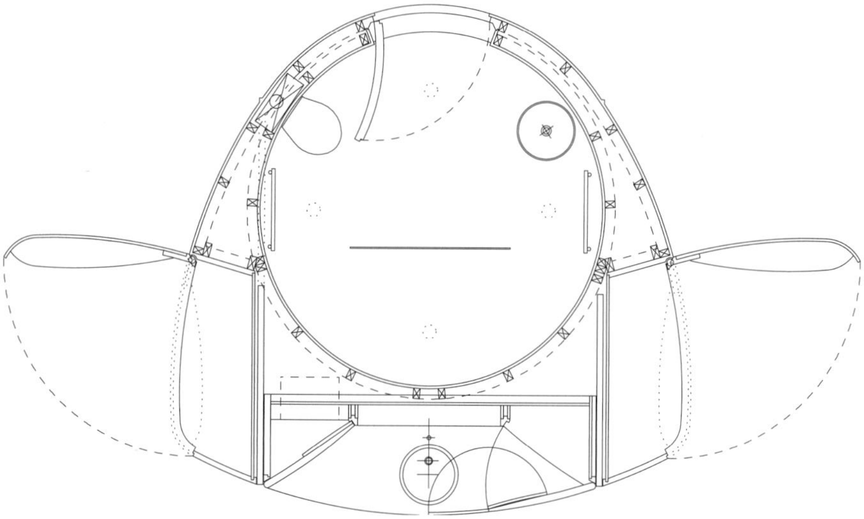

top plan of pavilion.

bottom left looking into and past the pod.

bottom right detailed plan of the pod.

opposite looking past the kitchen from one study to the other.

overleaf the pod.

The building lines of the new pavilion follow those of the original house, built 40 years before. The new pavilion is not a direct copy, it is a development and new interpretation. The south-facing cedar boards echo the boarding of the original house but are divided by narrow strips of glazing, creating dynamic light and shadow across the interior. The shallow asymmetric curve of the roof, whilst different, refers to the chamfered roof profile of the 1960s house. The roof of the new pavilion curves down at its western end and terminates in a spout to mirror that on the end of the original house. The two spouts cantilever out, reaching towards and nearly touching one another. Both spill their respective storm water via chains onto a circular array of stones. Our client commented that we "produced an inspiring design for the pavilion; it perfectly complements the unusual lines of the main house. The asymmetrical curve of the roof is exceptionally pleasing and from the other side of the valley it blends with the landscape so that the building is barely visible."

The new pavilion was conceived as a single barn-like volume, with a sinuous smooth plaster curved ceiling. Described by our client as "light and airy, it provides a comfortable and most attractive area in which to work." To achieve this feeling of unity and meet the brief, a free-standing pod was positioned at the centre described by our client as "a graceful design, which is hugely admired by all visitors and works well." A room within a room. The pod is a piece of fine furniture, incorporating a blood-red shower, toilet, storage cupboards and a small galley kitchen. Constructed from curved ply faced with selected weathered sycamore veneer, it has two large gull-wing pivot doors. "The large exterior cupboards are cleverly sculpted and offer most useful storage." A pair of bi-folding doors close over the kitchen counter to complete the pod's pure shape. Structural glazing runs over the top, so that when the sliding doors are pulled shut and the pivoting doors are closed, it divides the space both physically and acoustically. This glass is hung from the ceiling, and supported along its bottom edge by the roof of the pod. The idea is simple but the execution is complex and elegant. At either end of the pavilion are specially commissioned bookcases including open shelves and veneered sliding doors, making reading desks and hidden storage. These sliding doors are veneered with exotic timbers, individually selected and set out by us: "The use of wood, both structurally and in features such as the closed shelving, is outstanding, and is easy and sympathetic to the eye."

"The real achievement on the Manser Medal shortlist this year is the pavilion built in deepest Suffolk... which is nothing less than the English domestic ideal; the idea of home that is hard-wired into our heads."

— Hugh Pearman, *Sunday Times*, 22 June 2003

opposite meeting of the two buildings, new and old, gutter detail.

above looking past existing house to new pavilion.

opposite elevation detail of new pavilion.

right bookcase detail showing many selected exotic veneers in joinery.

ROBERT PARKER
SIEGFRIED SASSOON
WHO'S WHO 2000
Remember Nelson
WAR DIARIES
french

right joinery detail with view out to landscape.

There were two distinct processes involved in the making of the pavilion. The main contractor formed the overall weathered enclosure and studwork for the circular pod using curved ply templates, which enabled the shower, basin and toilet to be plumbed and programmed in at a sensible stage in the works. Meanwhile, a specialist joiner manufactured the curved outer wall, kitchen carcass and finely finished elements of the pod to the same curved ply templates. These joinery items were brought in right at the end of construction and fixed onto the builder's stud wall as the 'grand finale'.

Thinking about buildings in this way, as the making of forms constructed from materials assembled in a practical sequence to ensure elegant junctions, has to be a priority and leads to well-built buildings. Our clients express their "pleasure in the pavilion. Each time we enter we feel a sense of delight and an uplifting of our spirits. It is a truly beautiful building which we are proud to own." On completion the client held a party and gave every member of the team—designers and builders—a pewter mug engraved with the date and name of the project.

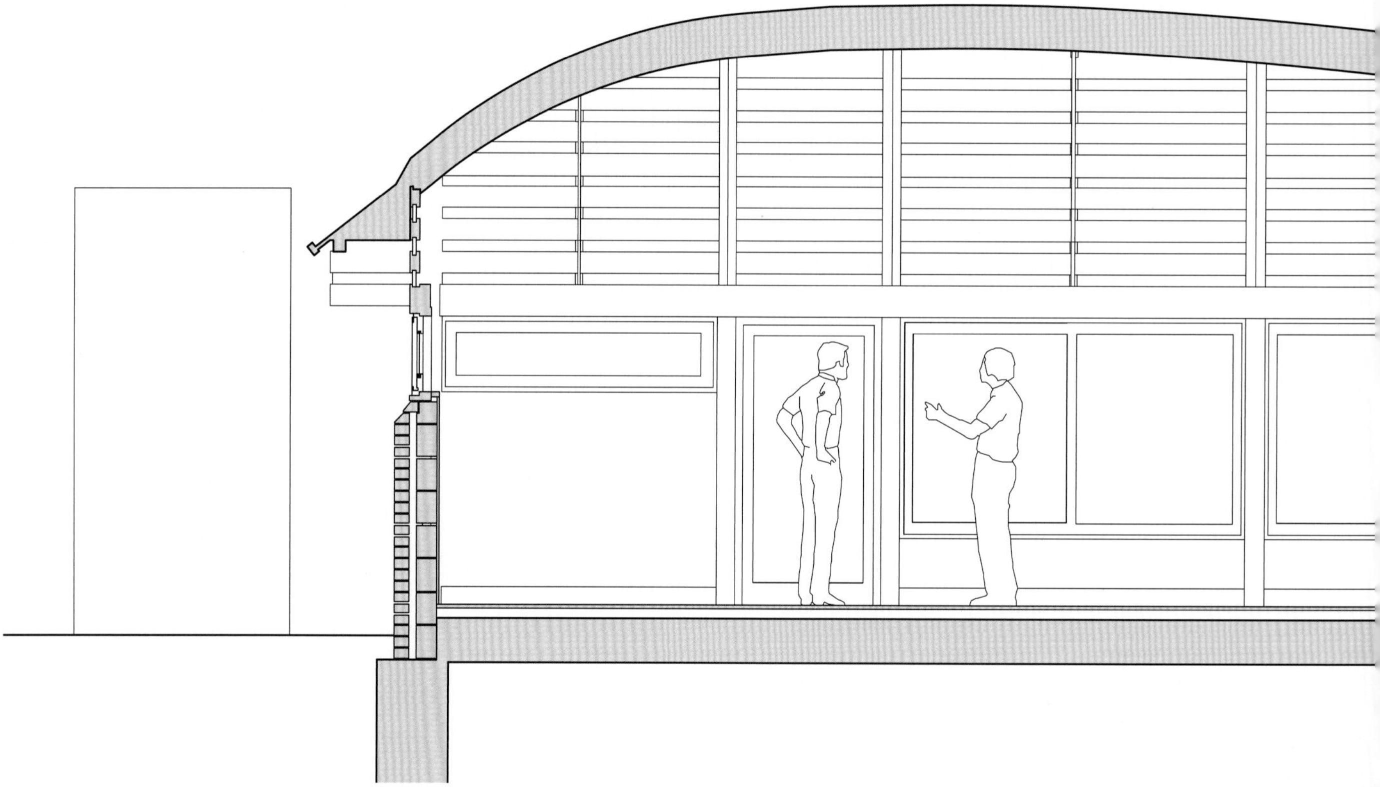

above long section.

overleaf view at dusk of new pavilion and original house.

This pavilion reflects much of what was learned by us at Hodges Place (Chapter two) about using joinery to form smaller spaces within a larger volume and the richness, warmth, colour and clarity that crafted joinery can bring to a space. A real synthesis of designer and maker is something we continue to grow and develop, enjoy and exploit.

New Maltings also forms part of a continuing narrative about a way of looking at architecture and building, of making powerful and interpenetrating space, using materials in a considered and constructivist way. A narrative started by Ted Cullinan, continued by Mark Beedle, followed by Sunand Prasad and with the latest addition by us. Who will be next? Like Hodges Place, New Maltings was shortlisted for the Manser Medal and although it didn't win, Hugh Pearman said of it: "The real achievement on the Manser Medal shortlist this year is the pavilion built in deepest Suffolk... which is nothing less than the English domestic ideal; the idea of home that is hard-wired into our heads."

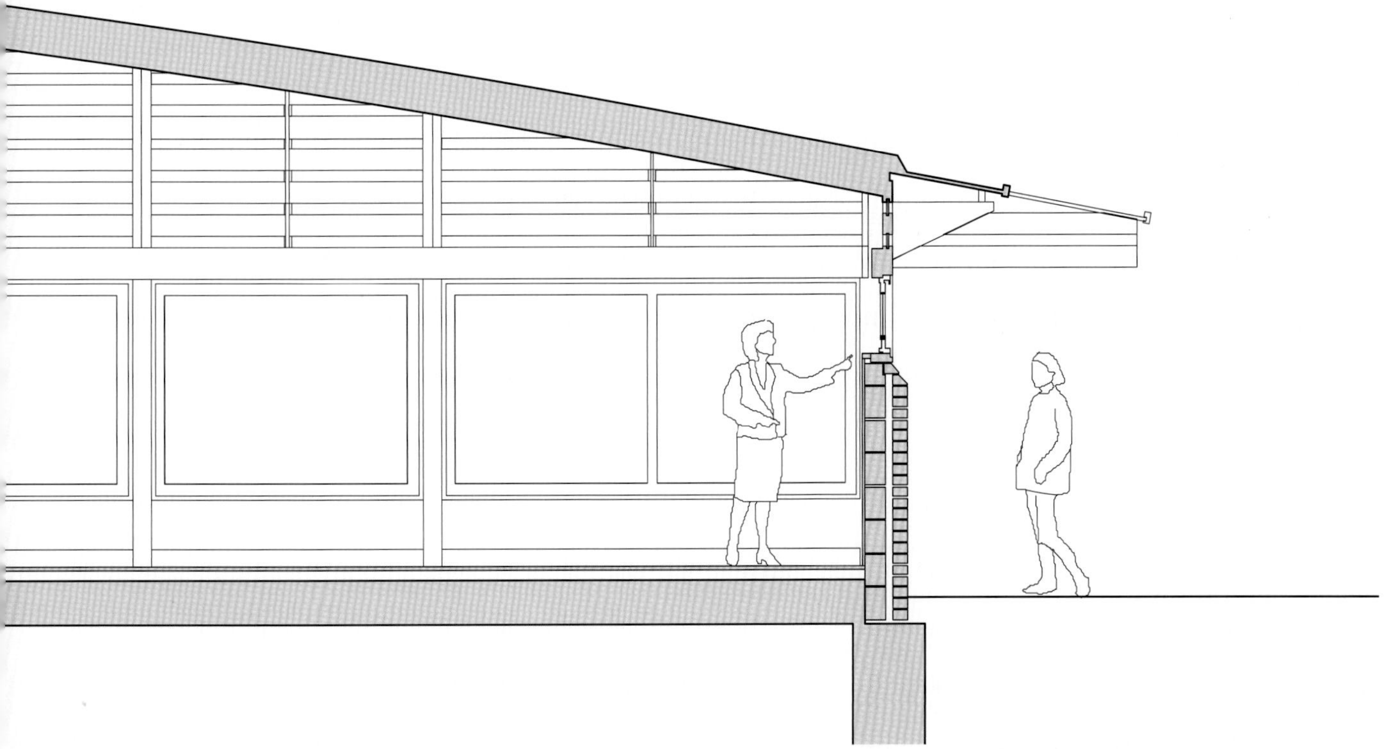

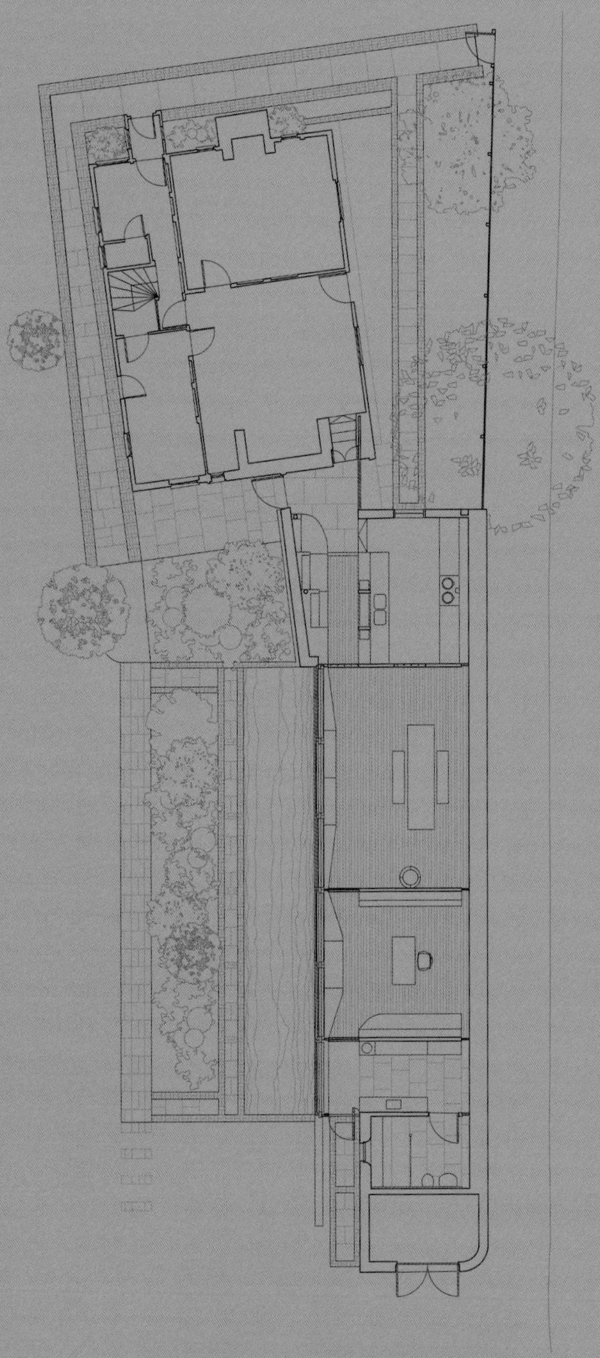

Chapter two

Old and New
Hodges Place
Offham, Kent, 2000

opposite the old house meets the new extension.

below view from garden.

In the sixteenth century, an old farmhouse with a catslide roof was built in Offham, Kent from the beams of a decommissioned warship docked in the nearby Chatham dockyard. Four hundred years on, in 1955 Alden York Miller (Sasha's maternal grandfather) saw Hodges Place advertised for sale in *Country Life* and bought it for £5,250.

Sixty-one years later (2016), it is now lived in by Maeve and Bhavan (Sasha's parents). For them, the sixteenth-century low-beamed rooms felt dark, disconnected from the garden and could not accommodate large family gatherings, or Maeve's creative writing workshops and University of the Third Age seminars. Because of this we were asked to extend the house in a way which would not detract from or diminish the historic house yet would provide a new kitchen, dining room and study, shower and boot room with space for the whole family, with a view of the long established and beautiful garden in all weathers. Discussions agreed it should be light, open and airy in deliberate contrast to the old Grade II-listed farmhouse.

The old house is full of memories, with its dark, sloping, wide oak-boarded floors, huge bowed oak beams, inglenook fireplace and crooked stair. It reflects the technology of the time when spans were limited to the size of available timbers, glass only available in small sizes and short supply, walls were poorly insulated and clay tiles fired only up to a certain size. It is built from a rich red brick, with mathematical tiles, local ragstone and a dramatic catslide Kentish clay tile roof. We felt a huge responsibility to maintain the dignity of the old house, but also to be bold and make something powerful and modern in its own right.

We wanted to reflect the life of Maeve and Bhavan. Married in Britain in the 1950s their mixed marriage was brave and forward-thinking, qualities to be reflected in the new building of Hodges Place. Maeve was born and brought up in rural Kent, but Bhavan's beginnings were very different as a Tamil who lived into his mid-20s in a village on the outskirts of Jaffna, at the northernmost tip of Sri Lanka. Bhavan's experience of life, food, climate and all aspects of culture was completely different. We had an opportunity in the new building to respect both ancestries. We had visited and enjoyed the Tropical Modernism of Sri Lankan architect Geoffrey Bawa, the natural materials and the use of water and reflection. Geoffrey Bawa's premise that "architecture cannot be totally explained but must be experienced" influenced us enormously.

The new construction barely touches the old building, allowing the old built fabric to stand alone. The new low-lying, single-storey building runs the full length of the Kentish ragstone kitchen garden boundary wall and has a grass roof. The wall facing the garden is almost entirely glazed with a full-length window seat running at the meniscus level of a 15 m pond just the other side of the window. The space is divided by sliding doors, allowing it to open into one long space. The dividing cherry-covered walls are detached from the ragstone boundary wall by fixed glazing, showing the ragstone running the full length of the new building.

"It is the detailing that lifts the extension out of the ordinary. The obvious would have been to have the stone wall at the back join with the ceiling, and the partition walls to abut straight onto the stone wall. Instead, we have a glass panel clerestory above the stone wall, lifting the ceiling away, letting more light in, and narrow glass panels between the partition walls and the stone wall somehow making the whole structure more delicate."

— **Maeve Bhavan**

opposite night view into new extension with pond.

overleaf view at dusk of new extension.

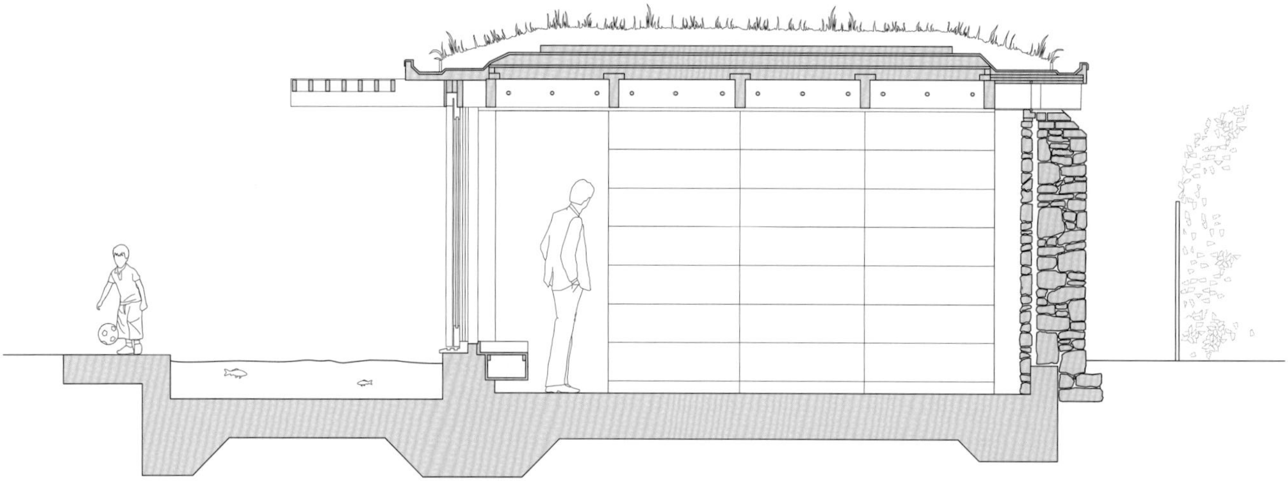

opposite top cross section through new extension.

opposite bottom morning view of dining room.

left detail of where window seat meets window and pond, with integrated oak heating grills.

right light filtered by the brise soleil and reflected off the water.

overleaf long view through dining room to landscape beyond.

The extension is made of self-finished natural materials used in a contemporary way. An inner skin of Kentish ragstone turns the existing boundary wall into an insulated cavity wall with steel frame posts set within the inner leaf. Oak-framed sliding double-glazed windows with concealed insulated aluminium roller shutters separate the window seat from the pond. Oak is used for purpose-made heating grills at window-seat level immediately below the windows. The brise soleil over the pond and the floor are also oak. The veneer on the dividing partitions is cherry, and ash is used for the ceiling panels. These ash panels sit within the Douglas-fir-strengthened structural steel frame. At either end are oak doors to the outside. We tried to demonstrate that a number of timbers of differing character, texture and hue can be used within the same space and result in a harmonious whole, complimenting and enhancing one another. Maeve said about the cherry wood panelling at the end of the dining room, "I appreciate the thought that went into the choice of cherry as the wood used, harking back to the fact that 100 years ago the garden was a cherry orchard." The boot room and shower have York stone floors. Fifteen years on, the floor has been refurbished but the walls, ceilings and other surfaces have never needed decorating. The new building, like the old, changes and improves with the patina of age.

When we built the pond Maeve said, "I welcomed the idea of having a pond alongside the extension, with the water surface roughly on a level with the window seat. What I had not anticipated was the delightful patterning reflected onto the ceiling of the extension to greet me on sunny mornings when I come down to breakfast."

It was a hands-on building project. We did not have a main contractor. Instead we employed and directed the workmen ourselves, with only specialist elements such as the steel frame being outsourced as discreet subcontracts. Bhavan supervised the day-to-day site works and Maeve fed everyone. Time and time again, we have found it is the people, the teamwork, the communication and the builders' enthusiasm for the job that make good buildings. Hodges Place was a great example of this for us. Grisha and Slavec, the site builders, came originally to underpin the existing Kentish ragstone garden wall ready for the new building to be placed alongside. They asked if they could do the whole construction.

Their first attempt at the stonemasonry was not bad, but we showed them exactly how we wanted the stones to be selected, mixed and laid in a more random way and the pointing to be recessed. The second attempt was a great job and they went on to build all the stonework inside the building, concealing the steel frame and insulation in the cavity wall. Similarly, with the site joinery this small team went on to do a good job and then complete the internal stone floor, the roof construction, the Erisco Bauder grass roof membrane and the mosaic tiling in the bathroom, much admired later by a fellow architect marvelling at such good mosaic tiling. The builders were methodical, not fast, but executed everything beautifully. Each week we described the next task providing drawings. Verbal communication was sometimes difficult and so our Polish plumber became our onsite translator.

"A detail I would never have realised the necessity for is the brise soleil. It doesn't merely add to the external appearance of the extension, it is also a very necessary feature as uninterrupted sunlight on the glass windows could have made the space very uncomfortable in hot weather."

— **Maeve Bhavan**

opposite shadows created by the brise soleil.

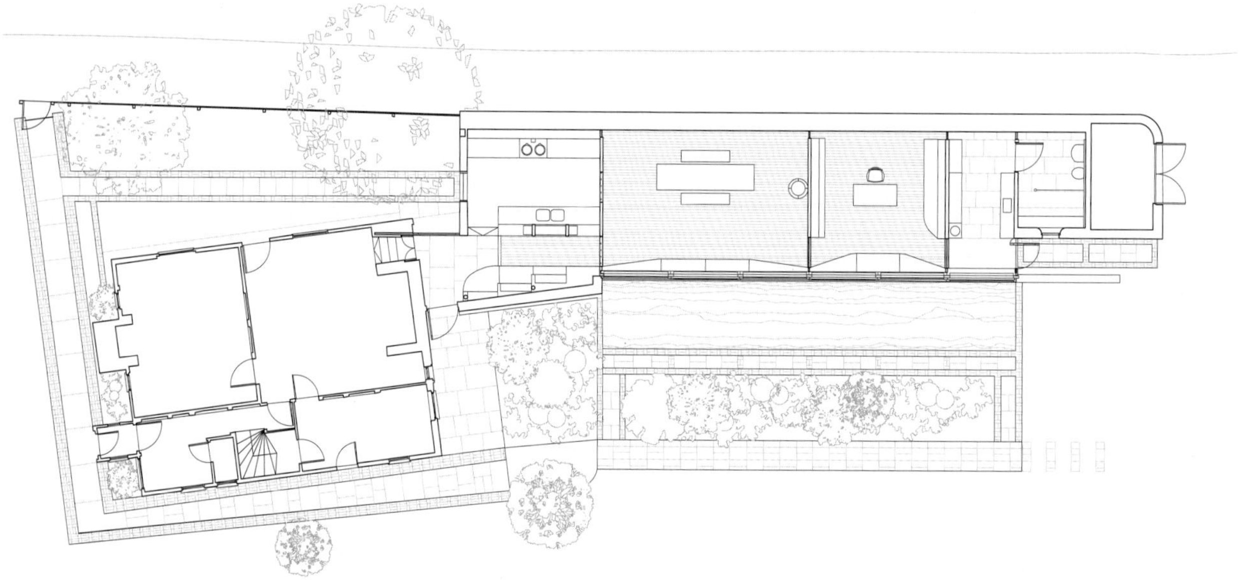

opposite top plan.

opposite bottom view from new extension to old house.

below view into kitchen.

The purpose-built joinery was supplied and fixed by Piper Products of Ashford. This is a joinery company we first encountered on a project where the contractor hadn't paid them and we were able to arrange for the client to pay them directly under the contract. They were used to making standard kitchen units and we challenged them to tackle bespoke joinery, which they did well. We built a good working relationship and have completed many projects with them. As Maeve says, "The built-in office furniture is a pleasure to use as well as to look at. All the hinges and drawer closings click nicely into place. I am aware that this sort of inevitable perfection does not happen unless created by an experienced eye." Perhaps most successful of all are the big windows above the window seats overlooking the pond. They can slide right back over each other in fine weather, totally altering the space; making the whole extension just part of the garden.

Whatever the time of day or year, sitting in this space looking out of the window is irresistible. It is a peaceful place when empty, and unbelievably jolly at Christmas and birthdays.

"Not entirely essential, but again a source of repeated pleasure is the mirror panels on the kitchen shelves, which create interesting images each time I pass." You cannot please everyone, though. Maeve's cleaner tells us every time we visit how much work these nonessential mirrors are to clean.

opposite the boot room.

above view from old house along length of new extension.

above cut-away isometric view of new and old.

overleaf midday view of new extension.

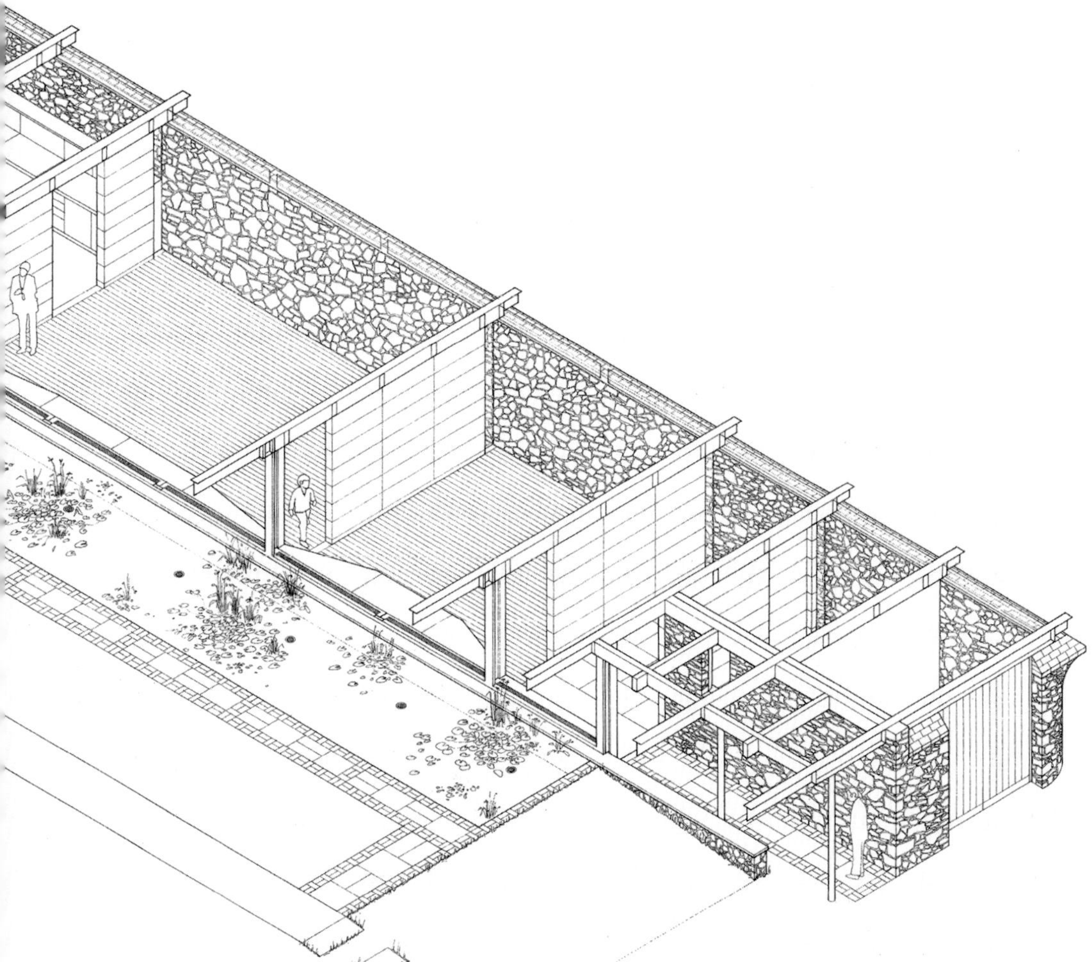

Chapter three

Many Levelled Bungalow
Crowbrook
Hertfordshire, 2013

Many Levelled Bungalow

In 2009, Mark de Rivaz rang us. He and his wife Bee were considering moving to a bungalow and single-level living due to Mark's rheumatoid arthritis and impaired mobility. They were both clear from the outset that they would not move again and that this house needed to cater for all eventualities. It was to be a house for them to grow old in, easy to get around in and be suitable for easy adaptation to wheelchair living. Their brief included throwing away all their furniture and many belongings and starting again with a clean slate. They bought a bungalow in a well-established garden and it quickly became clear that demolishing and building anew was the only solution. At a very early stage, Bee was clear about her intention to be ruthless about what would be acceptable in the new house. When the project was handed over we were delighted when she told us that, "If ever an architect brought together William Morris's two essential requirements—for objects to be both functional and aesthetically pleasing—it is you. We live in a beautiful home that works for us in every way." Mark had worked with us as Steward of The Bedford Estate, when he commissioned us to work with him to design the new Russell Square Cafe. He was familiar with us and our work so he asked us to come and look at the bungalow and see what could be done with it.

1 Kitchen
2 Dining
3 Living
4 Bedroom
5 Study
6 Utility
7 Shower / Bathroom
8 Plant / Store

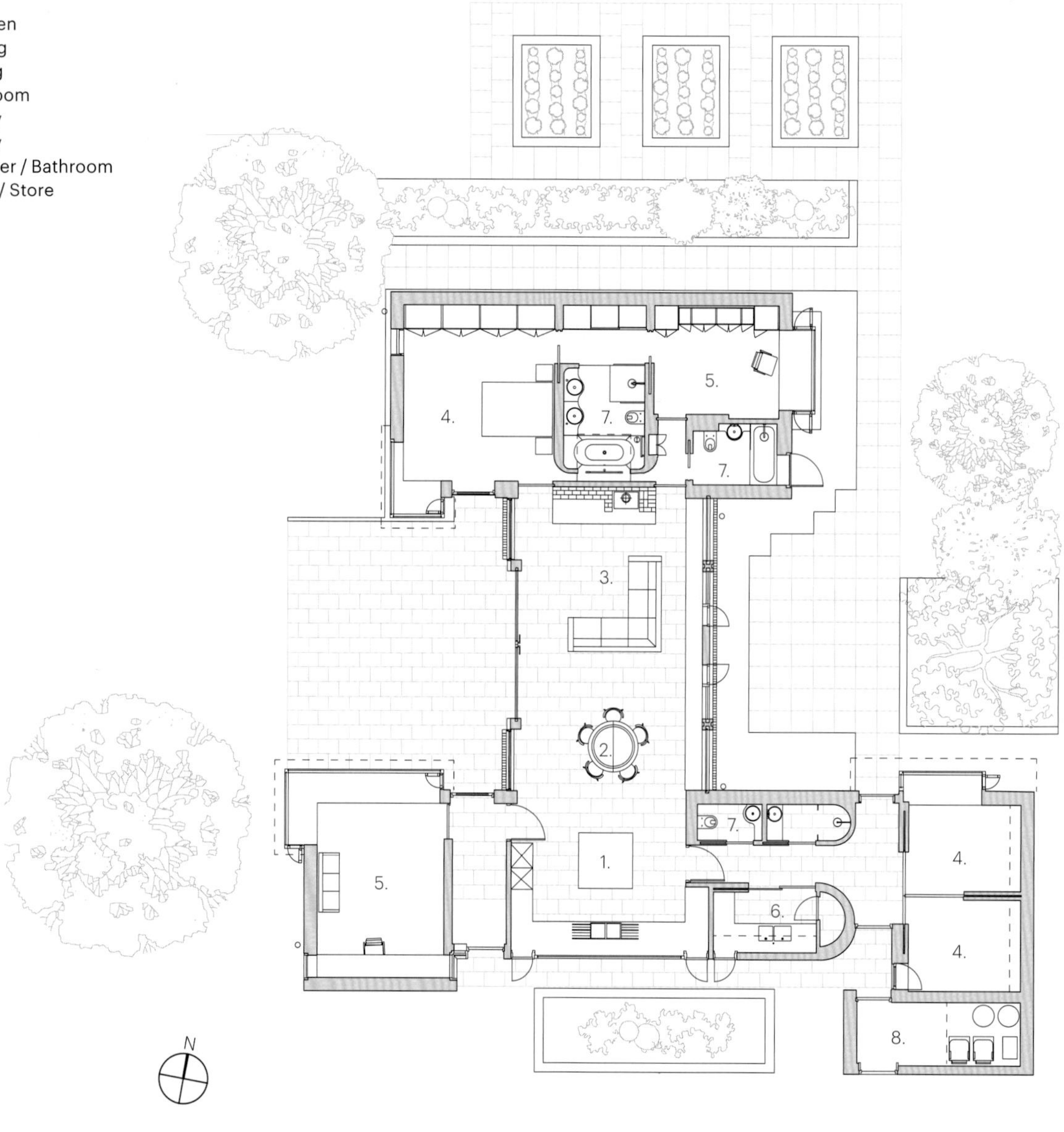

opposite plan.

above view from kitchen to main bedroom.

overleaf left kitchen.

overleaf right section through window seat.

"If ever an architect brought together William Morris's two essential requirements—for objects to be both functional and aesthetically pleasing—it is you. We live in a beautiful home that works for us in every way."

— **Bee de Rivaz**

Their village, designated a Conservation Area, meant planning permission would be tricky. But whilst the fabric of the old bungalow was poor, it had been designed in the 1970s by an architect and was well sited, so it was decided to build on the existing footprint.

The greatest challenge of the project was to imagine how Mark and Bee live now and would live in the future, and for this to inform the design. Their old house covered many rambling levels and contained numerous rooms and quirky places; the new house had to think ahead, move away from a traditional closed layout of corridors. Privacy was not a driving force now. It was more important to be able to use and enjoy all the space whilst having space adaptable enough to have family visits. We achieved this by making spare rooms only just big enough for a bed and a suitcase, and by using sliding doors which could be left open when unoccupied so that all the space can be seen and enjoyed. Sliding doors blur the edges of space and create long views through the house.

The site at Crowbrook is flat. A house on a sloping site has a ready-made gift of drama and movement; a multistorey house has the potential for double height spaces, stairs and ramps, balconies and galleries. However a house set on a single level on a flat site is a challenge. Is this what makes the ubiquitous bungalow so often boring? Crowbrook became a many levelled bungalow designed to be experienced sitting, standing and lying down. The fabric has an embodied discipline of levels. Built into the interior cladding are levels of window seats, desks, countertops, window soffits and ceilings. A standard ceiling height of 2.4 m runs throughout the house, until you reach its heart where the house breathes out and the ceiling rises to 4 m. Up at 4 m, the windows make contact with the sky and catch the light from north, south, east and west to bounce it down through the space below.

The contrast between the 2.4 and 4 m ceiling heights provides scale and drama. Down at 2.4 m, the ceilings run uninterrupted into the bay windows, expanding the perceived space. RIBA judges commented that it is "A house with a mid-twentieth-century feel... easy to spend time without feeling the need to escape... the roof pops up to form a tower allowing high-level windows to bring daylight into the heart of the house... [it] brims with natural light."

Crowbrook is designed for everyone and not specifically for disability. In a wheelchair you share an eye level with children and, provided openings are wide enough and windowsills are low enough, everyone can enjoy the space. Disability can often mean moving is painful, exhausting and takes time; long views connect you to both the house and landscape beyond. Removing corridors or circulation space can enable you to see through spaces, out to the garden and the sky, reducing any sense of claustrophobia and lifting spirits.

There is a deliberate view directly into the heart of the house and the kitchen from the main bedroom. When recovering from an operation, the last thing Mark wants is to be stuck away in a bedroom far from the action. This way, he has a grandstand view lying in bed. Although completely internal, light floods into the main bathroom through a large roof light. While lying in the bath, Mark can look out at scudding clouds by day and stars by night. For comfort and economy, the house is extremely well insulated, has low-temperature underfloor heating throughout, solar panels and a planted green roof. To date, the energy bills have been about £200 per year. Bee said that we "had the expertise to show us where to spend and where to save, without compromising on the end result, which is absolutely beautiful".

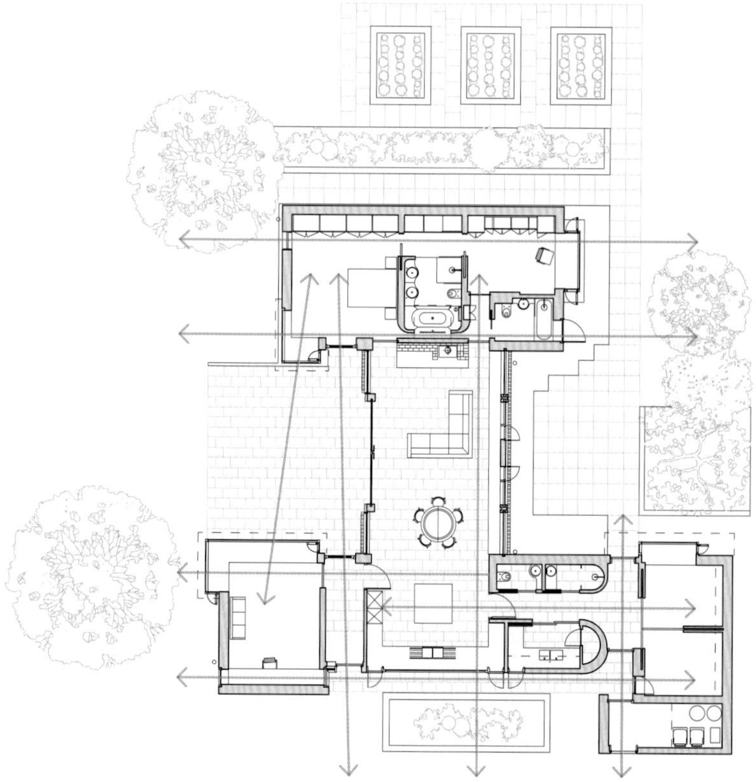

right plan showing views through building.

opposite winter view out to garden from dining area.

left looking from main bedroom into sitting room.

right long view through sitting room to kitchen; study window seat seen through window.

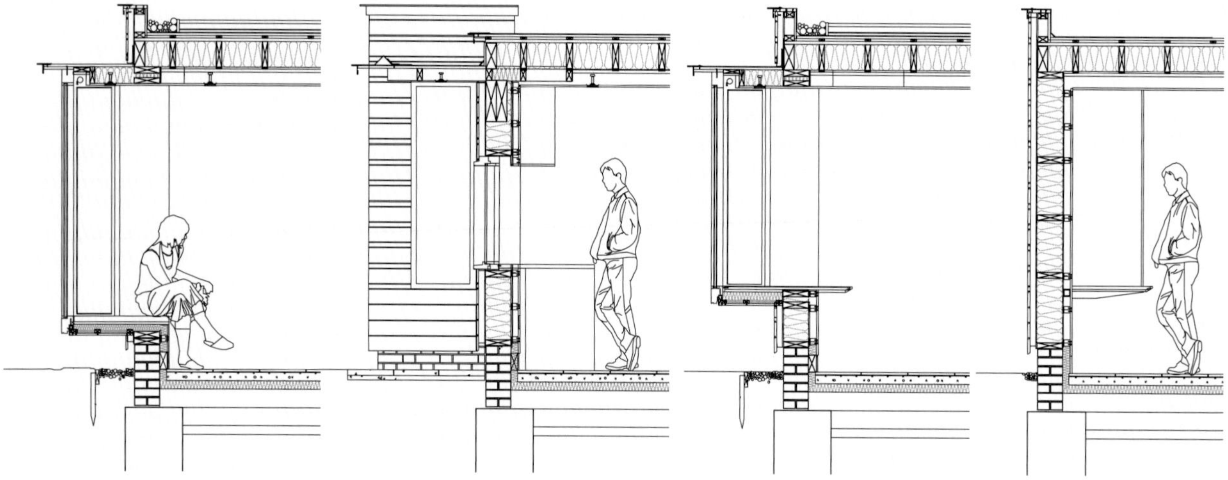

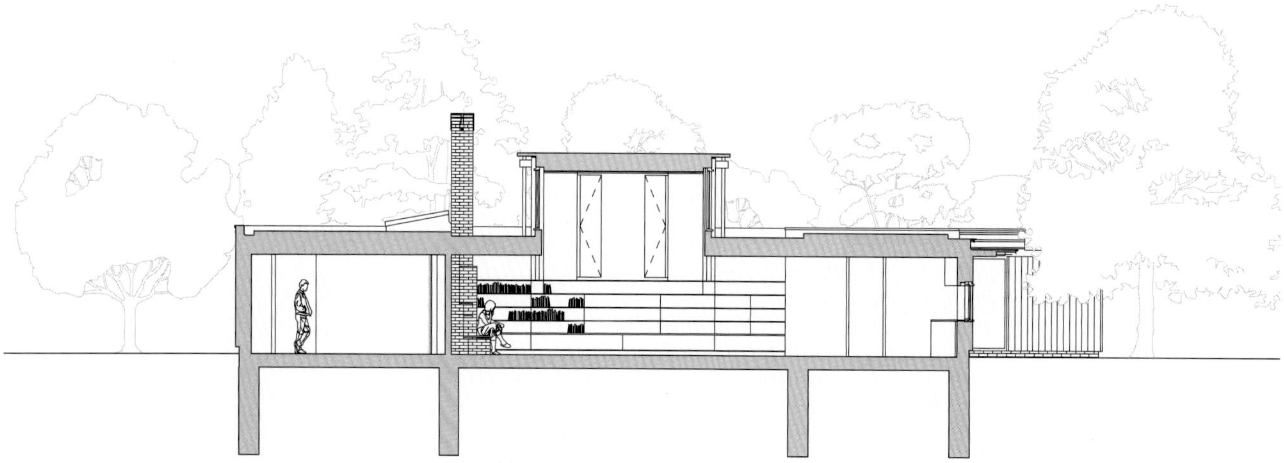

"A house with a mid-twentieth-century feel... easy to spend time without feeling the need to escape... the roof pops up to form a tower allowing high-level windows to bring daylight into the heart of the house... [it] brims with natural light."

— **RIBA Judging Panel**

opposite top sections showing co-ordination of cladding—window seat, kitchen counter, desk bay window, study desk.

opposite middle west, garden elevation.

opposite bottom section through main space showing roof 'popping up'.

above rooflight over bath.

To combine elegance and a generous view of the garden the bay window seats are cantilevered. Their glazed corners hover over the ground, bringing lightness and delicacy to the design. To achieve the maximum area of glazing and minimum obstruction frame, the glass is fixed whilst solid shutters open to provide ventilation. Coordinated black larch cladding is set off by a pre-patinated green copper parapet drip. These natural materials weather well and sit easily in their village setting. However, we discovered that black cladding on a south-facing wall moves significantly and we had to adjust the tolerances.

To describe the building process, the main contract was split to separate the timber frame from the main contract. The intention was for the timber frame to be designed, shop drawings approved and fabricated ahead of time. This meant that the frame would be ready to come straight in once the main contract was let, saving time. In the event this was not what happened. The timber frame fabricator did not perform. The frame was late, inaccurate, out of plumb and badly built. What came out of the disaster was unexpected and, as our contractor Gavin says, "we could have all stood there and argued" but "everyone stepped up to the mark, architect, client, QS and us. We worked through the problems together...." Having said that, he "will never do that again, where a package is outside our control" and neither will we.

"Everything about the job was collaborative and you don't get that very often, do you.... It has been a very good project for our portfolio... the building looks lovely, I want to live there."

— **Gavin Charles, Builder**

left construction photo—timber frame being erected.

right front elevation.

opposite large sliding double doors to garden with cedar-slatted brise soleil.

"Every aspect of our house does exactly what it's supposed to do... [you] had the expertise to show us where to spend and where to save, without compromising on the end result, which is absolutely beautiful."

— Bee de Rivaz

Gavin found the process one of "give and take". "It wasn't an adversarial builder vs architect relationship at all and the client was kept part of the decision-making process throughout. We all worked together, the Quantity Surveyor, everyone.... Despite the structural frame problems and the complicated glass all the elements came together.... Everything about the job was collaborative and you don't get that very often, do you?" Finally, Gavin says he enjoyed the experience, "It has been a very good project for our portfolio... the building looks lovely, I want to live there."

Such a good relationship with the client builder and design team is not always a given, so we were particularly proud when our client recognised our role as key to the success. "Sasha's attention to detail was scrupulous", they added, "... every aspect of our house does exactly what it's supposed to do. It is "a deceptively simple design creating something simply beautiful".

Having worked with many respected architects in his role as Steward of the Bedford Estate, Mark was particularly delighted when architect Rab Bennetts visited Crowbrook and said:

> You have created a really wonderful house and are rightly very proud of it. So many people in your situation would have reverted to something more traditional but the spatial flow of modern design is irresistible! It also looks great from the outside.

opposite view of the study window seat from garden.

right view of the study window seat from house.

overleaf view from garden in winter.

pp 74–75 view from garden in summer.

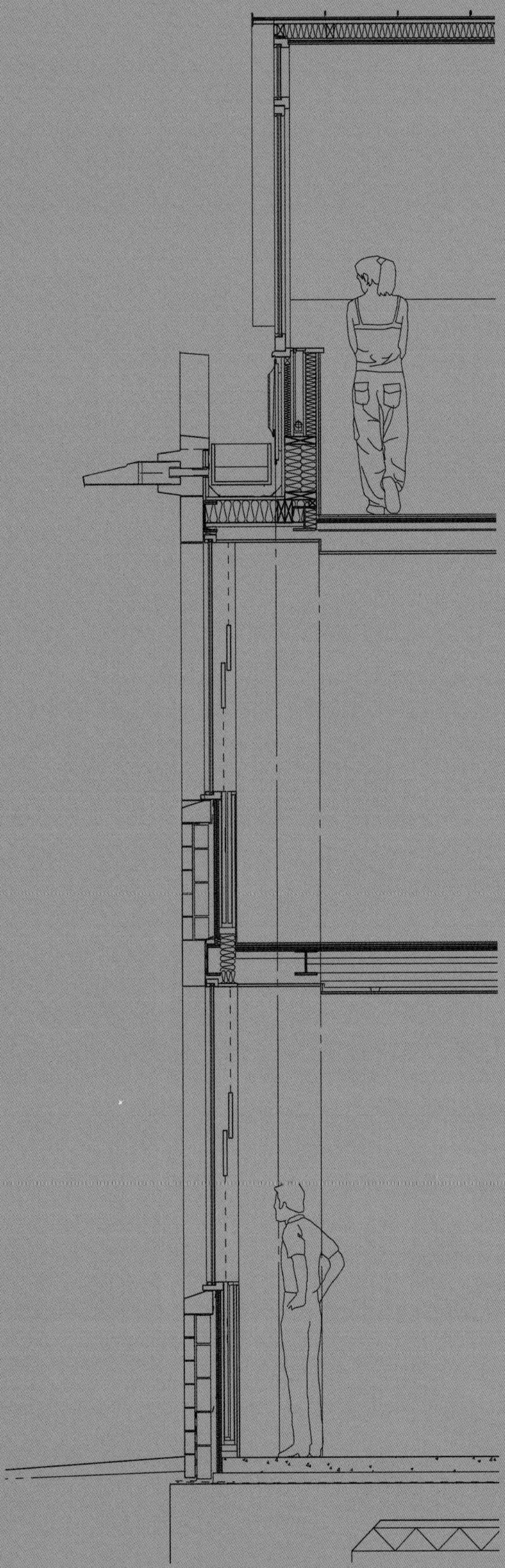

Chapter four

"A Missing Tooth in the Smile" — Eleanor Young
Brownstones
Dulwich, London, 2014

"A Missing Tooth in the Smile" — Eleanor Young

Greg and Jenny Falzon bought an ugly 1950s house built on the site of two terraced houses damaged by bombing during the war with the intention of demolishing it and replacing it with two houses to complete the terrace again. Their brief was clear in that they wanted something modern but which also reflected the surrounding Edwardian architecture.

Eleanor Young described Brownstones as, "A missing tooth in the smile of a long terrace of pretty Edwardian houses", which really captures the original intent of this mirrored pair of infill terrace houses. We wanted Brownstones to be as much of its time as the Edwardian terrace it sits in, bold and brave, not polite or fashionable but gutsy, full of character, solid and secure. It is similar in scale, rhythm and function to the existing terrace and at the same time playful and rich in materials and composition. The materials are natural and robust; red and cream sandstone echoing the colour and composition of the red brick and white stucco either side.

The two front doors are brought together under a single welcoming arch whilst the windows immediately above are pushed back to create dramatic, deep reveals separating the bays from one another. The carefully detailed solid stone and curving gable gives the front elevation richness without the Edwardian stucco decoration. The playful rainwater spouts are the exception about which Greg says, "I am quite fond of them as they confuse passers-by". Careful detailing of the materials, to create bold shadow, light and colour, characterises this elevation. As the client says, "Although our house is nonstandard / bespoke, it is incredibly functional and we do use pretty much all of it. There aren't in our view any very fussy or twiddly features and that was a strong aim from the original brief."

"Our house is above all our family home. It is of a high quality and flexible and functional—we use all of it. It has a consistent feel and quality throughout rather than occasional, attention-seeking features."

— **Greg Falzon**

left construction photo—front spout.

right detail of front door.

opposite front elevation.

overleaf view along street.

31
33

pedder
LET BY
pedder

The many miles of Victorian and Edwardian terraces throughout our cities have two very clear faces: the polite, dressed up, public street elevation and the private, unadorned rear garden elevation. At Brownstones, the rear elevation departs from the traditional brick of the existing Edwardian houses either side. It is clad in timber, which sweeps up onto a slate roof without a visible gutter, and the detailing of small repetitive elements such as timber and slate make the elevation tactile, more of a scaly skin than a wall. The smooth curve where the roof meets the wall below bounces uninterrupted light down into the ground floor kitchen, which we felt was an important design feature. This detailing, however, was challenging for both the client and builder and not easy to achieve. Greg commented that whilst "the curved roof brings more light down into the kitchen, it was a source of great angst with builders and building control".

"The curved roof brings more light down into the kitchen, it was a source of great angst with builders and building control."

— **Greg Falzon**

opposite timber clad rear elevation and covered terrace from back garden.

left construction photos—curved ridge and timber backing for slate hanging.

right view from kitchen to garden terrace showing rooflight.

The paired rear extensions took an enormous amount of work to get right: three floors were created where normally there would be two; and in plan, the awkward rhomboid site geometry was pulled back to a right angle using quirky bay bedroom windows. As Greg says, "The rooms at the back of the house are more successful than we imagined. We feared they might feel a bit stingy, but they are fine and the deep window sills and window seats help by scooping precious space out of the walls." We achieved a sense of light and space, despite the narrow deep plan, by being able to see right through from one end of the house to the other. Greg and Jenny are very aware of this "calm open space filled with light. We are often struck by this when returning home after having been away."

Light comes from all directions, including from above, over the kitchen. A compact, top-lit and simply detailed stair makes the most of the available space, reducing circulation to the minimum. The polished walnut handrail feels warm to the touch, its naturally glossy deep colour contrasting with the painted balustrade. On the street side, the bay windows at ground and first floor levels are a modern take on a traditional Georgian detail where a pair of timber shutters pull up, using a weighted box sash system, from a box concealed below the windows. These can cover half or the entire window depending upon how the owner feels. The clients appreciate the way that "the shutters on the front windows are very effective and flexible at modulating light and summer heat and stowing neatly into the sills." Other details within the house particularly appreciated by the clients are the large doors that sit flush in the walls between semi open-plan spaces, which "are great for keeping everything clean and allowing us to switch between different arrangements without it feeling that there is an open door flapping about half of the time."

right detail of stair.

opposite top second floor plan.

opposite bottom first floor plan.

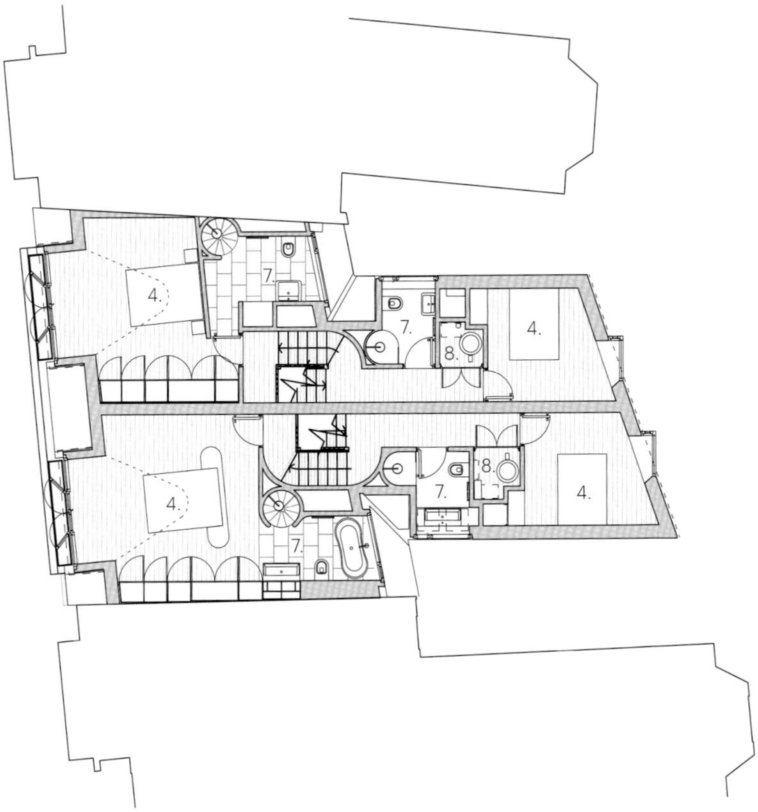

1 Kitchen
2 Dining
3 Living
4 Bedroom
5 Study
6 Utility
7 Shower/Bathroom
8 Plant/Store

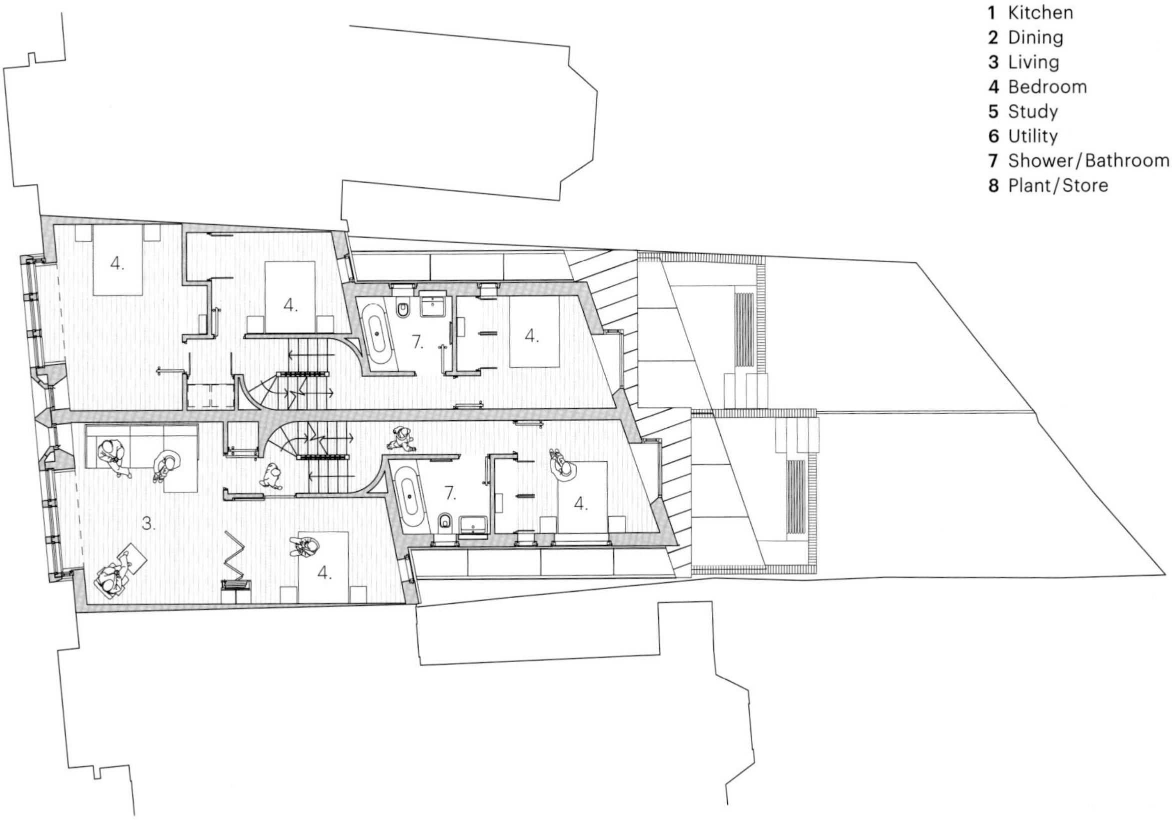

1 Kitchen
2 Dining
3 Living
4 Bedroom
5 Study
6 Utility
7 Shower/Bathroom
8 Plant/Store

When we asked the clients what single item they found was best value for money they, said the "mirrors throughout to magnify the space and add interest". This is something we find appreciated by clients over and over again: the light and the changing views created by mirrors and their reflections.

The bedrooms have bamboo floors, chosen for their quick-grow sustainable credentials and the ground floor is polished concrete—a raw, hard-wearing, self-coloured, easily maintained material. The client said that "the material choices, particularly the flooring, contribute to a simple, calm and unified feel." A Corian kitchen worktop stretches out through the glass end wall into an outdoor room, a covered terrace of hard surfaces with a built-in bench and steps up into the garden of plants and grass. The clients love this when it is raining.

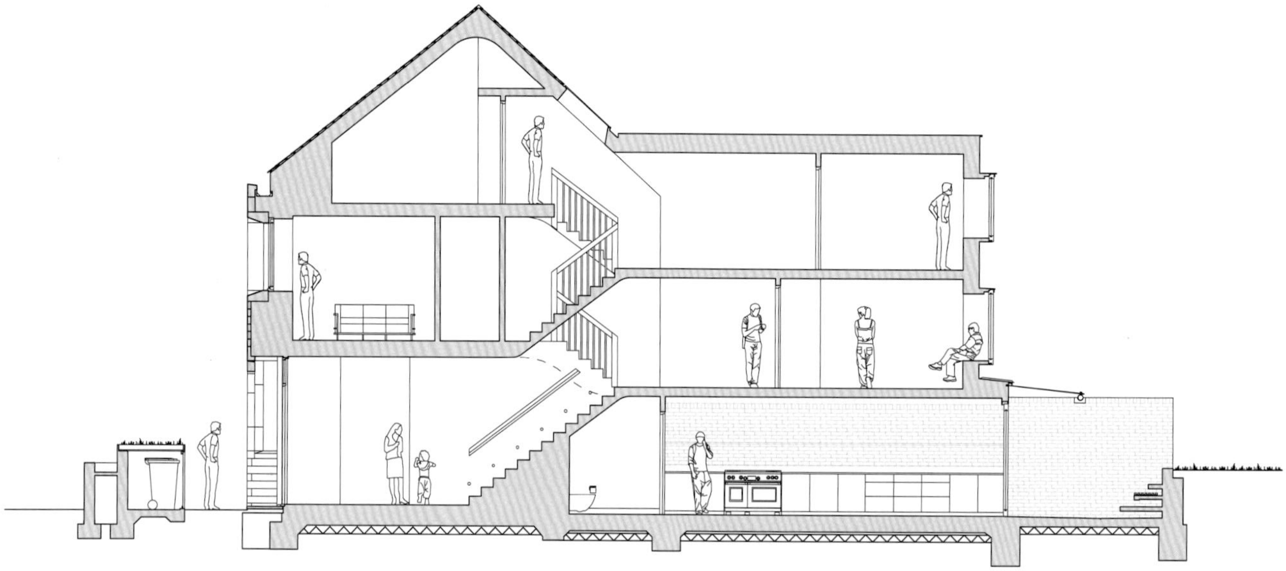

"The rooms at the back of the house are more successful than we imagined. We feared they might feel a bit stingy but they are fine and the deep window sills and window seats help by scooping precious space out of the walls."

— **Greg Falzon**

top long section through stairs.

bottom detail of bay window shutters.

opposite view from top landing.

The site is irregular. The plan attempts to iron out the anomalies so that the tricky geometry is not perceived or disturbing. As the client points out, "We have a wonky site (our house is an irregular rhombus) in plan but the various triangular shapes have been concealed internally so it feels like a normal flowing space without there being bits that feel like they are residual." This was achieved using the curved stair walls, levering window seats out of the rear facade and tucking curved baths into the tight corners. The success is that you don't notice it.

Greg is right, it was not an easy site and they were not easy houses to build. The first builder pulled out halfway through the project. A list of contractors had been drawn up, one of which we had worked with before but the rest came recommended. The chosen contractor was one we had not worked with before but was impressive at interview and appeared to understand the project, which we all knew was complex. Once on site, however, they couldn't reach the standards we expected. They pulled out and left us with a half-finished building.

"The curved ceiling in the master bedroom is lovely and the way the shape catches the light in different ways means there is always a contrast of shades."

— **Greg Falzon**

left sliding doors and glass canopy creates a seamless transition from garden to kitchen.

right view from sitting room to kitchen.

opposite ground floor plan.

Greg then found a new builder, recommended by a friend of a friend. He understood the challenges and rose to them, starting by checking the waterproofing and the wiring, and pressure testing the plumbing. The first builders had not built to the tolerances required. Things were out of plumb and had to be rebuilt. The second builder, Dennis, liked our drawings and how detailed they were. He loved working on the project and when the project was finished he took his mother-in-law and all his family round to see his and his team's work. It has proved very useful to him as an example of what complexity he can achieve and for getting more work. With hindsight Greg commented:

> A learning point for me is that I would put greater emphasis on choosing a builder that an architect had worked with before and therefore knows what they are getting into.... An hour of interview is a good way of selecting someone that has prepared well for interview, but this is no substitute for having worked together over a period of months.

Again our experience is that the most successful projects are always the result of good relationships and an enthusiastic collaboration between the builder, architect and client. Greg's final comment to us was:

> Our house is above all our family home. It is of a high quality and flexible and functional—we use all of it. It has a consistent feel and quality throughout rather than occasional, attention-seeking features. It has started to adapt for us as our family has begun to grow—we have just put the boys together in their 'suite' with adjoining playroom so that we can reclaim a study at the top / back of the house. I am able to sit and write this at my desktop Mac at the back of the lounge whilst 'looking after' my boys by peering intermittently through the window to the kitchen.

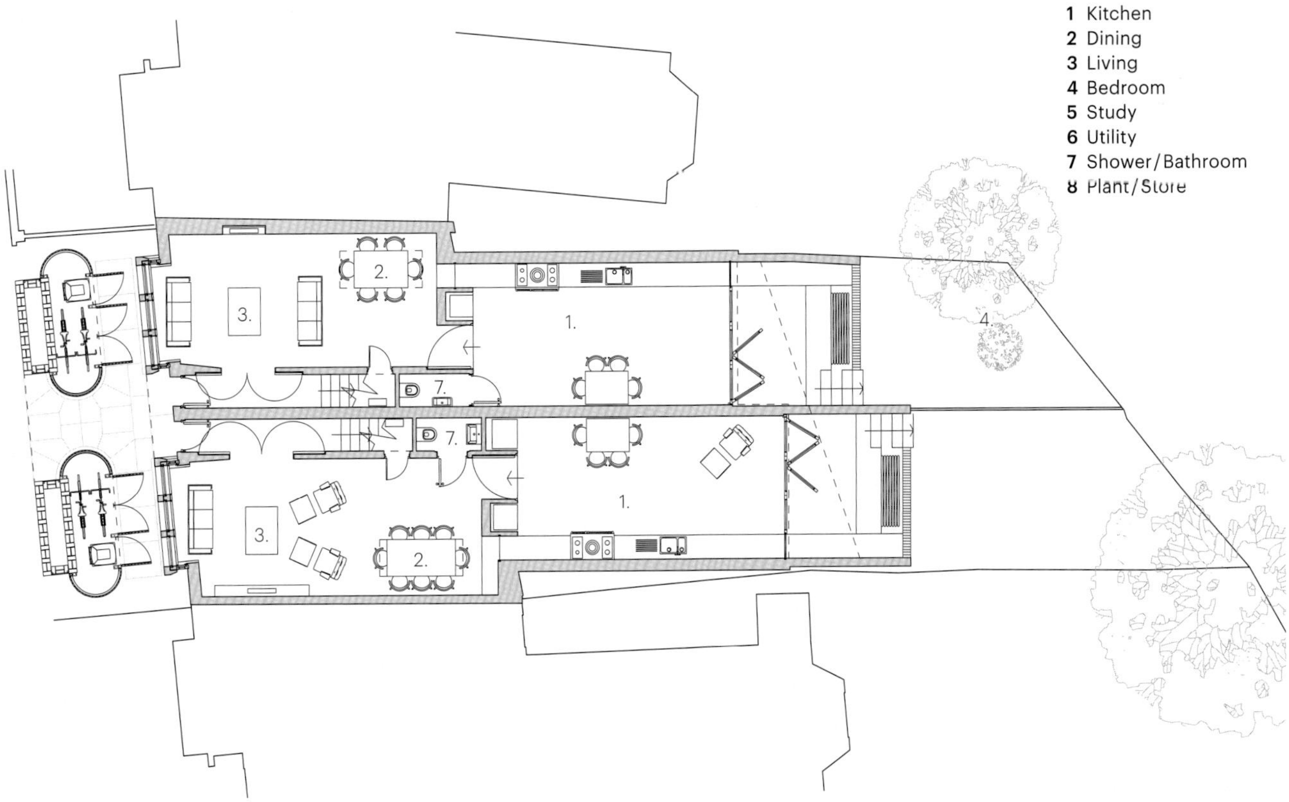

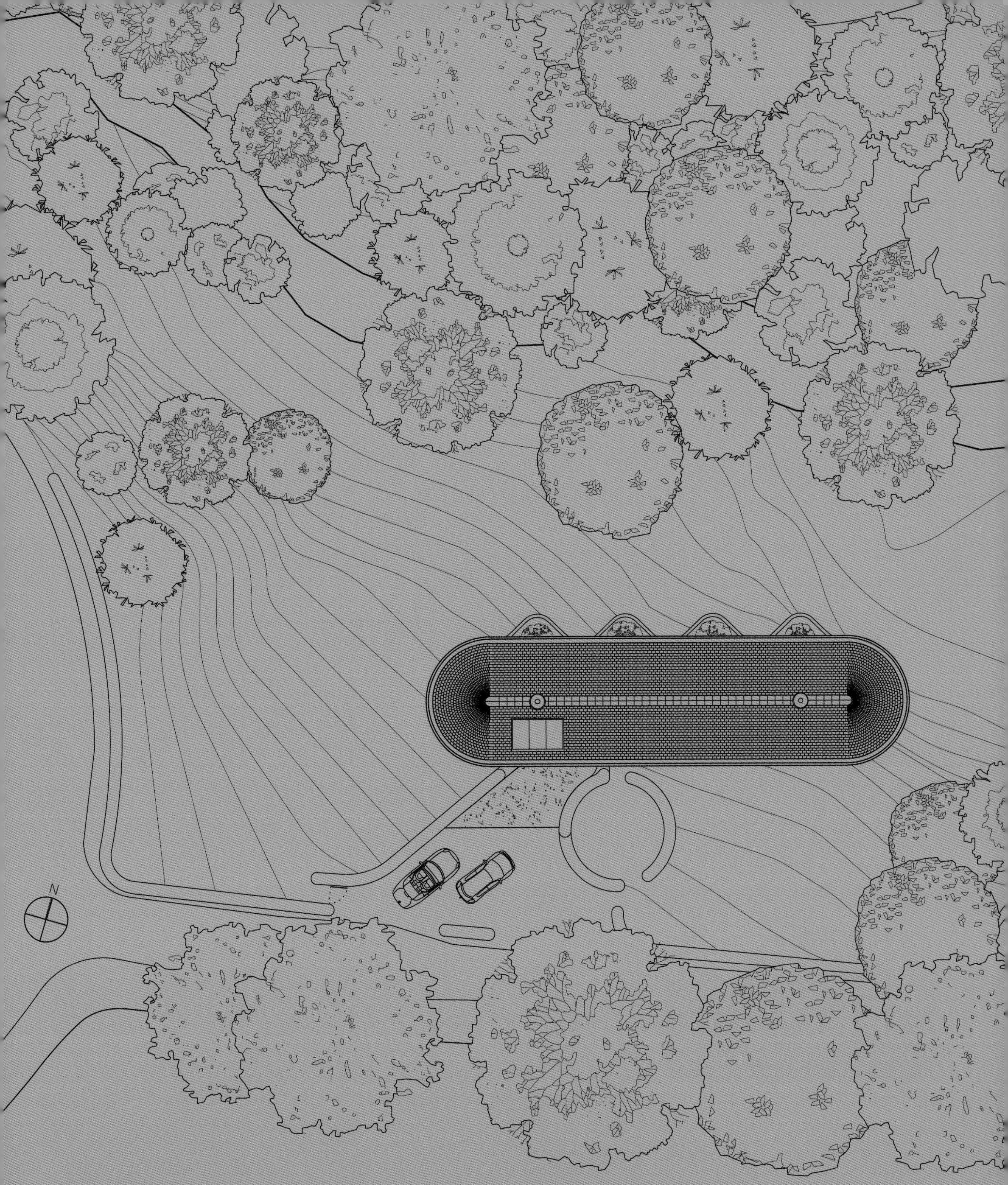

Chapter five

Building in a Single Material
Rigg Beck
Lake District, 2011

Building in a Single Material

Rigg Beck replaced the 'Purple House', a well-known house in the Lake District, where, amongst others, Sylvia Plath and Ted Hughes used to stay. A Canadian, Victorian kit house, the Purple House was timber framed with lath and plaster walls inside, lapped timber cladding outside and no insulation between. It fell into complete disrepair some time ago, with holes in the floors and roof. The site is spectacular, set within an acre of the tightly controlled Lake District National Park, just off the Keswick to Buttermere Road. Remote and far from any other dwellings, it was only possible to build on because the Purple House stood there already. The day before our outline planning application was lodged with the Lake District National Park, the Purple House was burnt down, making local BBC news. Local youths had long used the house as a place to drink and smoke, and a smouldering cigarette end on a summer evening led to the early-morning fire.

Our clients Charles and Jenny Carter had bought the house and site at an auction held at the local golf club. Although the room was heaving with people, only four had come to bid. Jenny's elderly father lives nearby and this was to be their eventual retirement house. They took time to choose us, spending "considerable time talking to a wide range and number of architectural practices over six to nine months to understand their approach, their experience". They wanted "a design sympathetic to the site which, while meeting the demands of the planners, was 'of our time' rather than a pastiche of existing local styles, understated rather than brash and meticulously considered". Charles's background in engineering figured strongly and he liked our approach, thinking about construction and materials from the outset. When asked recently about the experience of working with us, they appreciated "the regular and extensive discussion between us" and said of us that "they had a willingness to listen and adapt while, at the same time pushing [their] point of view if [they] had thought it was right, which is one of the things we paid for! [They] were responsive and engaged us in all the necessary decisions. It was an enjoyable process and there is no doubt that [they] were deeply committed."

left the original, now demolished Purple House.

right view of Dale Head from Rigg Beck.

opposite winter view of house under construction.

overleaf new house looking across to Cat Bells.

On our first site visit we decided that the house should not sit at the west end and top of the site where the burnt-out Purple House stood, but that it should run down the hill perpendicular to the contours and parallel to the beck. Each elevation was to face a landscape of different character. To the west, set above the site, is Causey Pike, a neighbouring fell; to the north the beck is surrounded by tall pines; to the east is a view of the landmark fell Cat Bells, often sprinkled with snow. Finally, to the south is the gentle rolling valley grazed by sheep, reminiscent of a world described by Beatrix Potter. It was this southern view, up the Newlands Valley to Dale Head, which would be the primary view from the main living space. The simple form of the house and its roof responds and reflects the profile of Causey Pike above it. As it runs down the hill more floors emerge, until the east end of the house where it is three storeys high, its ridge centred on a line drawn from the top of Cat Bells a mile to the east. This enables the principal rooms to collect south light and enjoy views.

An early design decision was to construct the house out of principally one material: locally sourced slate. It was divided into three bands: a dry stone walling plinth, slate wall hanging and a slate pitched roof with a continuous narrow clerestory window running around under the eaves of the roof, disengaging the slate roof from the slate wall below.

"A design sympathetic to the site which, while meeting the demand of the planners, [is] 'of our time' rather than a pastiche of existing local styles, understated rather than brash and meticulously considered."

— **Charles Carter**

right Rigg Beck.

opposite top construction photo—slates laid on apse-end of roof.

opposite middle tapered cylindrical slate chimney stack.

opposite bottom ground floor plan.

The dry stone walling plinth is 225 mm thick Burlington slate cladding from the South Lakes laid 'watershot' (tilted down towards the outer face). The slate hanging on the roof and both walls is reclaimed Westmorland slate reportedly from a hospital in Newcastle—it must have been a large building, as a considerable quantity of slates from the same source were needed for Rigg Beck. The vertical walls and pitched roof are both clad in slates laid with distinctive diminishing courses where large and thicker slates at the base reduce to small and thinner at the ridge. This is a traditional detail in Lake District vernacular, and is a way of minimising wastage. It requires considerable skill to build. We worked with the local slater to get it right, ensuring that the laps and diminishing courses agreed and that the joints or 'perps' were staggered and did not coincide.

The chimneys are tapered cylindrical slate stacks, which counterpose the long horizontal form of the house. We went through heartache over the detailing of these chimneys to achieve hidden flashings, leaving nothing visible. The blockwork core is dressed in lead flashing then clad in diminishing courses of slate stone walling. No visible flashing means the stone appears to descend cleanly into the building at either end of the main living space. The clients recognised that Knox Bhavan "design to a much greater level of detail earlier than many and, as a result, [they] had a much greater confidence that the design would work out as well as [they] want".

The views up the valley to the south were all-important. To get this view you have to be able to see over the wall of the adjoining field. To make absolutely sure that even when sitting down you could see the view, we mocked up a platform on an early site visit, standing and sitting on it to reassure ourselves that this was the optimum level to see the view from. Facing this view, glass fins project at right angles from the house. These fins have inlaid mirror stripes acting as a brise soleil for low sunlight from the east and west. They provide some wind protection, as well as casting dramatic and aesthetically pleasing shadows. Although not strictly essential, the client lists these as one of the things they would definitely not have left out. They tell us they love the combination of framed views, the sense of space and the fact they can stay snug while the weather does its worst.

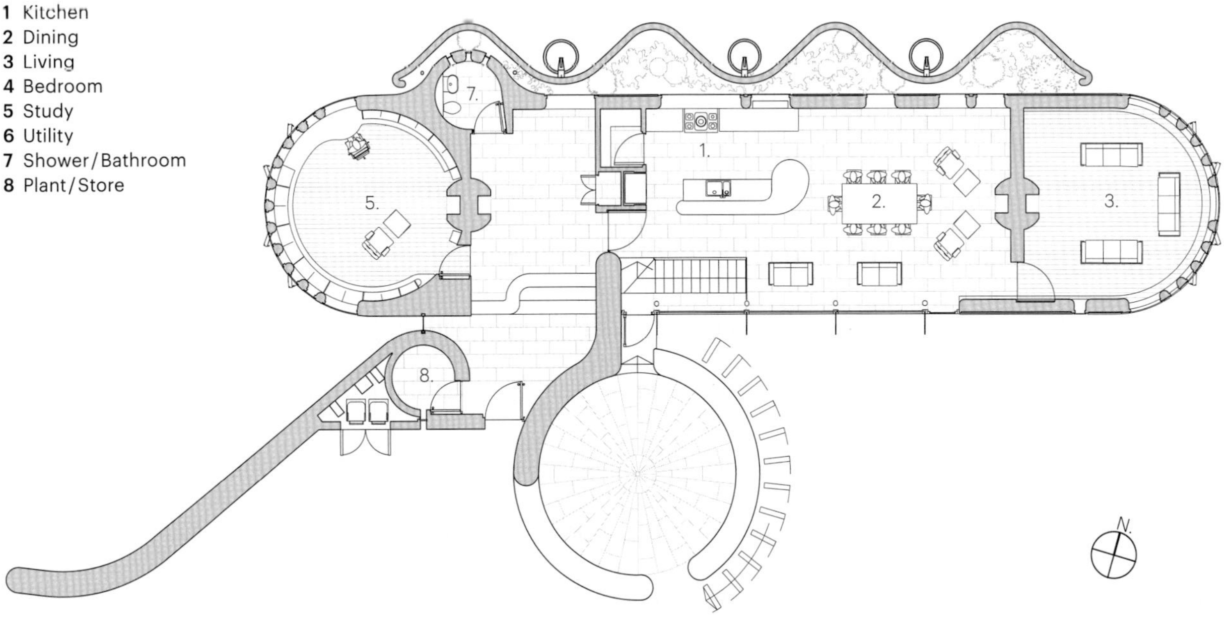

The undulating form of the north wall responds to the shape of the beck cutting its way down through the site. The angled bays give each bedroom views up and down the stream. The upper section of this wall is covered in larch cladding responding to the woodland setting it faces. The setting out of this cladding had to be exact. The internal perimeter distance of the boards sets out both curves and boards. Templates were made to ensure that the dry stone walling below sat perfectly within this line. The stone walling also had to be very accurate. Above these bays are green roofs planted with ferns suitable for the north-facing aspect.

top left construction photo—window/tile hanging joinery shop mock-up.

bottom left detail of timber bay facing Rigg Beck.

right detail showing timber bay with slate wall below, slate hanging and chimney above.

opposite detail view of the house from the beck.

overleaf view from the beck of north face of house.

opposite Rigg Beck with its purple door alluding to the Purple House.

top view of surrounding landscape.

bottom view looking down on the house from the west.

A number of shaped dry stone walls lock the house to its surrounding landscape. An angled dry stone wall supports a flat porch roof and links the front hardstanding with the front door of the house. The roof of the porch is planted with purple heather and the front door is purple too, in memory of the old Purple House, which stood on the site before. We were advised the boundary walls needed to be 1.5 m high to prevent sheep jumping over. One ton of stone was needed for every linear metre.

A circular dry stone wall forms a sun terrace, an outside room on the south side of the house, with the top of the wall being planted with herbs. This curved enclosure contrasts with the rectilinear form of the main house. This form was inspired by the curved dry stone walls of Andy Goldsworthy. Inspired by the same Goldsworthy walls, a 'moon door' or circular opening has been made—using carefully set out thin slates on end—in the stone wall leading to the outbuildings (garage and shed), making a route and visual connection between them and the house. A cylindrical ply template was used to support the slate arch as the circular opening was being built.

"[You] design to a much greater level of detail, earlier than many and, as a result, [you] had a much greater confidence that the design would work out as well as [you] want."

— **Charles Carter**

opposite left construction photos—
building the circular stone opening.

opposite right view of house from
garage and wood store.

above curved terrace wall with
Causey Pike behind.

opposite mirrored glass fins create dappled light.

top left detail of base of wall on apse.

bottom left detail of circular sun terrace.

right detail of circular Lazenby red stone surround, set into slate dry stone wall.

Five years on when asked how the house was working for them, Charles and Jenny replied that the unexpected delights were "the way natural light plays in the house, changing through the seasons—helped by the mirrored glass in the fins and in places where you don't expect it, eg from the round windows and the GRG [Glass Reinforced Gypsum] plasterwork". We find mirrors are repeatedly mentioned as an unexpected bonus. Charles reported back that they wouldn't swap "the mirrored kitchen units (Jenny is now totally convinced)" and that they appreciate most of all "the sense of space and light".

"The way natural light plays in the house, changing through the seasons—helped by the mirrored glass in the fins and in places where you don't expect it, eg from the round windows."

— **Charles Carter**

above view looking south to Dale Head from kitchen.

When asked what advice they had to give others, Charles and Jenny's response was:

> First, don't be rushed. In general we weren't, and had the time to think. Our major error was when we found we needed to do a significant redesign to accommodate budgets, we rushed it, persuaded by the fact that we had a contractor ready to go.... The advice is, do take time, don't be rushed and remember that architects' fees, while not insignificant, are minor in terms of the whole cost. (And consider employing a clerk of works.) Second, make sure that the house is easily maintainable. Planted roofs need weeding and must be easily and safely accessible; windows need cleaning and need to be reachable; gutters need clearing and it has to be possible to put a ladder up to them safely; and light bulbs need replacing, which is tricky when they're high up in the middle of a domed roof.

Rigg Beck took 18 months to build, starting on site in 2009 and finishing March 2011, covering six seasons and two winters. Site visits meant leaving home at 4.45 am to catch a 5.30 am train, finally arriving on site at 10.00 am. Leaving site at 5.00 pm to catch the 6.00 pm train meant arriving home at 10.00 pm. Moving between such different worlds was an experience. Particularly memorable was arriving in the Lakes and being unable to get to site because of the floods. In heavy rain the water runs off the fells in sheets and spouts through the holes in the walls as though they were colanders. The labourers and tradesmen were proud of being hardy and able to work through all weathers. When sites down south had stopped for bad weather we would find the men in Cumbria still working in far worse conditions and perishing temperatures. The winter of 2009 was particularly harsh but work never stopped.

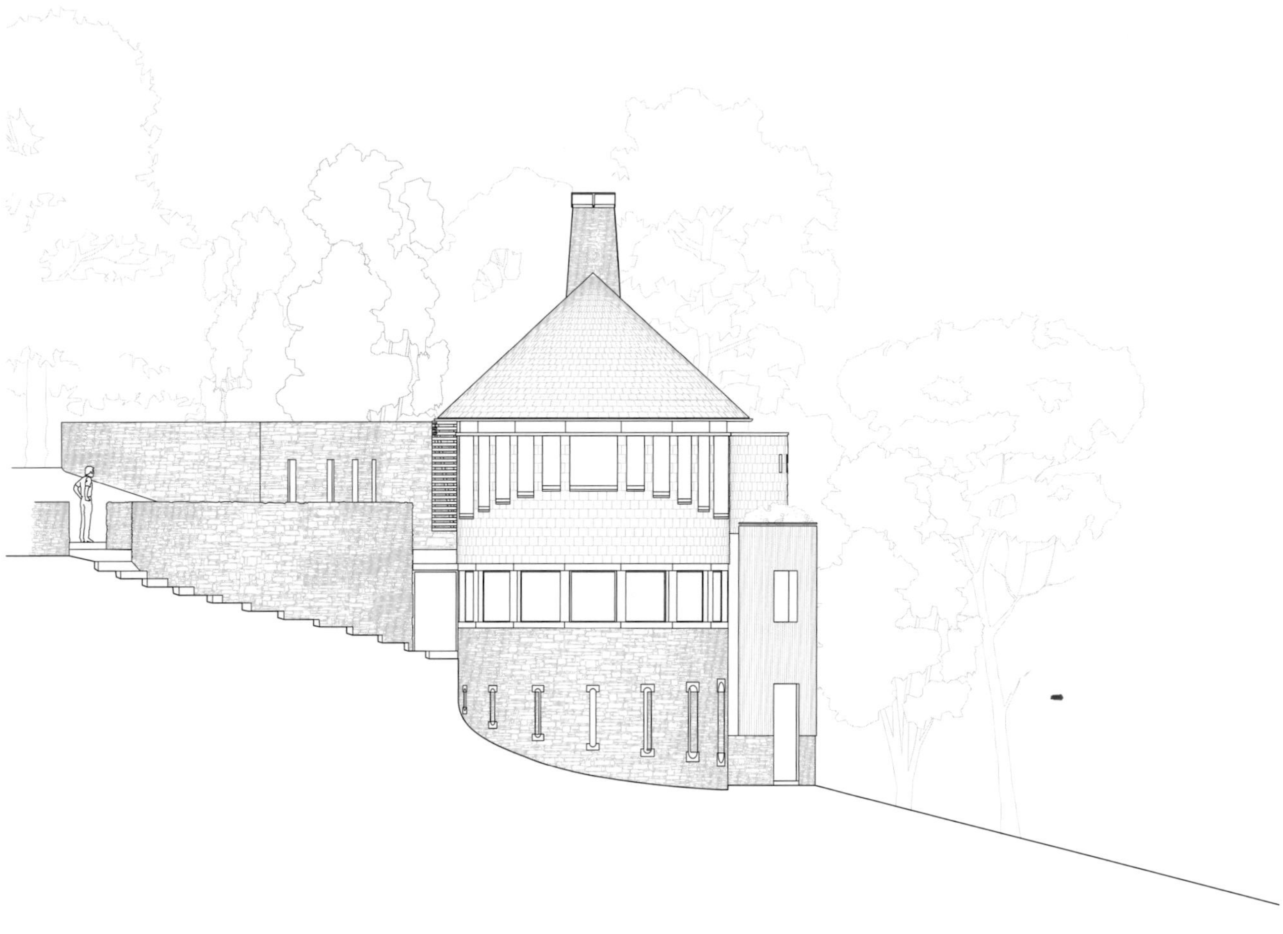

For every site visit we made throughout the year during rain, snow or shine, Vic (the waller) was laying the stone walling around the house. He was a man aged beyond his years by constant exposure to the weather, and he had had a triple heart bypass. One day when we visited the site, we noticed that Vic wasn't there and we were concerned that he might be ill. We were told, "One thing you need to know about Vic is that walling comes second to showing his prize sheep at the Westmorland County Show!"

"We wouldn't swap the mirrored kitchen units... and we appreciate most of all the sense of space and light."

— **Charles Carter**

opposite east elevation.

left construction photo—building a dry stone wall.

right detail of kitchen Kirkstone slate counter top, looking towards study.

above south entrance elevation showing diminishing slates on roof and wall hanging.

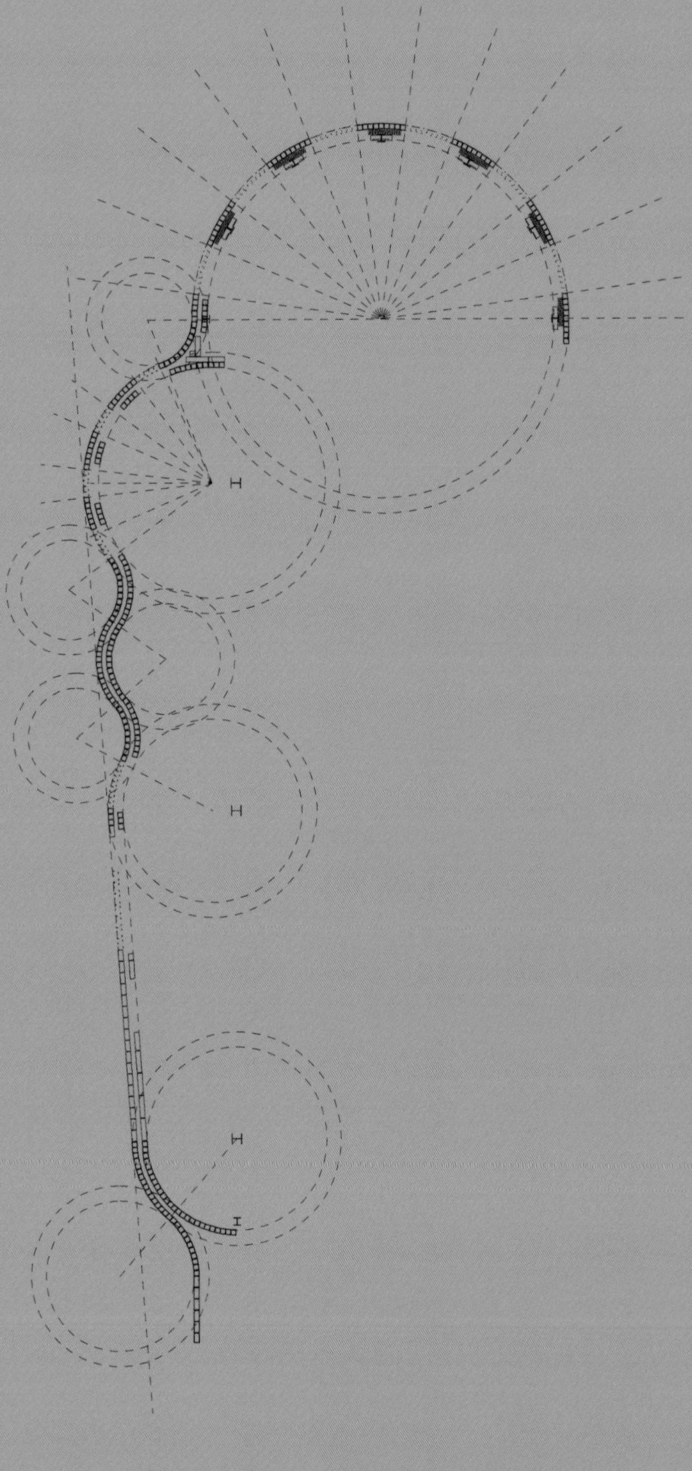

Chapter six

"Even a Brick Wants to Be Something"—Louis Kahn
College Road
Dulwich, London, 2009

"Even a Brick Wants to be Something"—Louis Kahn

The commissioning of a new house by a client involves trust. Trust that their designers and builders will spend their money wisely to meet their brief and create something they could never have imagined or executed alone.

We were on holiday in France when we were surprised by an unexpected call from an old client who rang to tell us that, although not looking, they had found a site. They were living in a house renovated and extended by us and were very happy, not intending to move. However a perfect potential site had come up and with four growing children they needed more space, and being antipodean, a modern house was really their ultimate dream. They also said that it was only because they had been through a building process with us already that they "felt confident enough to even contemplate embarking on a substantial new build". Planning permission for a small house on the site existed, but for it to work for the client we needed permission for a larger family house. They made an offer to buy the site and the first step was to test the water with the Planning Authority and The Dulwich Estate (the site is located on estate land) who set some ground rules.

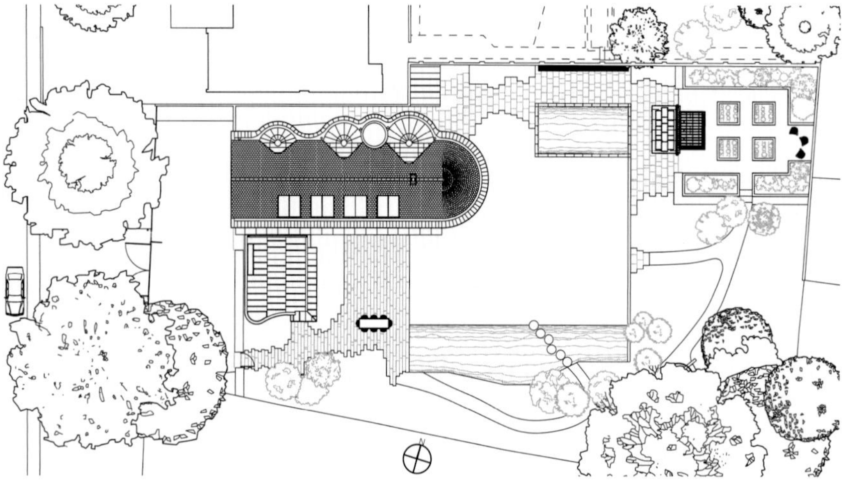

left site plan.

right view showing seamless transition from inside to out, from kitchen to garden.

overleaf view of house from garden.

The Dulwich Estate stipulated that the house should not face the road but "turn its shoulders—side on" to it. Advice from the planners and the estate together with the site and the client's brief gave us a framework; ground rules to respond to and, if necessary, to challenge.

After initial investigations we set about designing the house with our client. Our existing relationship meant that we had an established and successful way of working together. We had an in-depth understanding of their needs, desires and way of living whilst they had an understanding of the way we work.

Most important of all was that the inside should have a strong connection to the outside. The orientation of the house, views of the house from the new garden and views of the garden from the house were all-important. The result was to make the garden an extension of the house, creating more space for living by blurring the thresholds with internal floors running straight outside.

The plan and section of the house are simple and easy to understand. The main house has two storeys above ground with a basement and a pitched roof. The family bedrooms and bathrooms are upstairs and the main living space at ground level. Below ground the basement has a wine cellar, games room and extensive storage space. The house sits on the north boundary of the site turning its back on next door. Set at right angles to it on the road boundary is the single-storey guest wing. This is deliberately private with its own access to the garden, a favourite place because "the garden comes into the house in the guest bedroom with its door out into the garden and its glass corner, and the bathroom is beautifully top-lit."

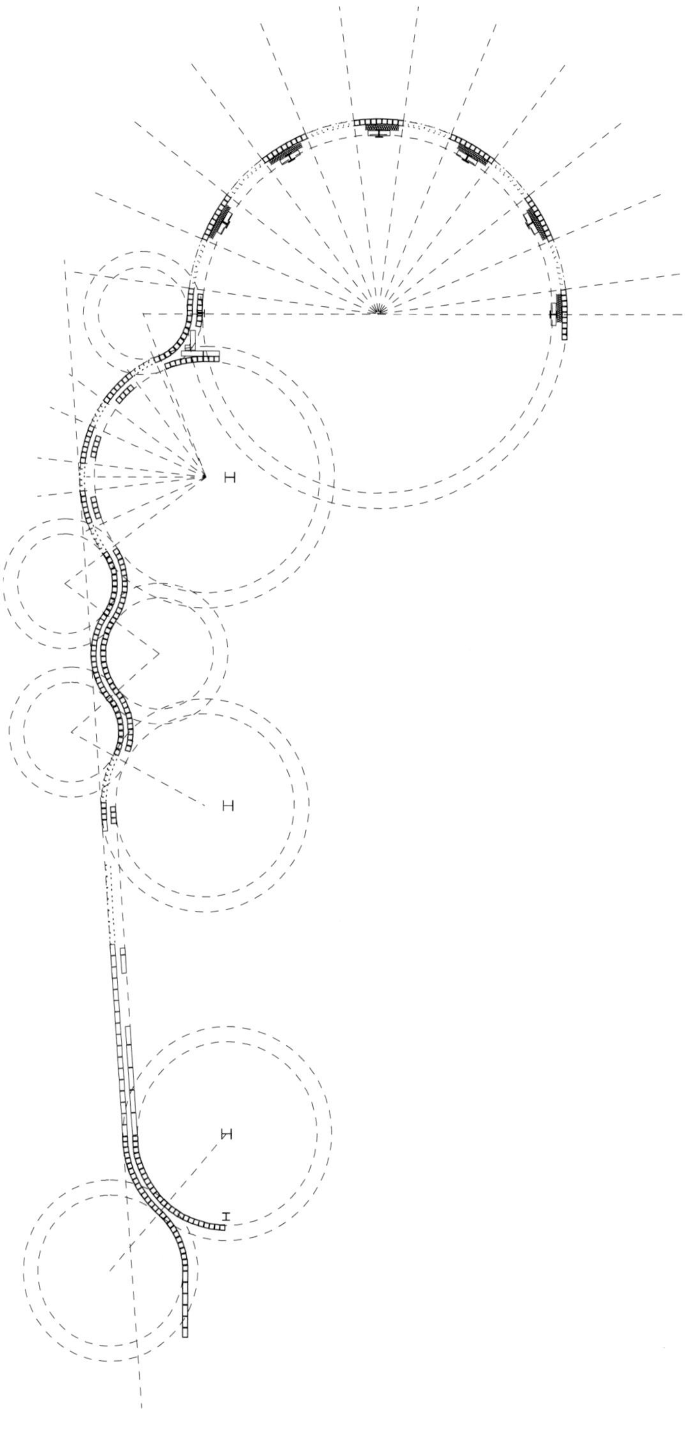

left construction photos—brickwork setting out templates and construction of curved walls.

right plan showing brickwork setting out.

opposite first floor plan.

Each of the four girls were to have their own bedroom, with the guest bedroom located well away from the family bedrooms giving privacy for long-staying Australian relations. Living accommodation was to be as flexible and interconnected as possible with some space for teenagers and young adults to hang out away from the rest of the house. Pre-empting sibling rivalry, the four girls' rooms were identical. The girls themselves however are all very different and as their mother says "we can't generalise, they are so different; two live in their rooms and two don't. Their relationship to their rooms has changed as they grow up but they all love the volume of the rooms, the bedroom desks and window seats (although they fill these with clutter!)."

This client values the way our buildings are visibly constructed from recognisable materials, put together in a practical, controlled and informed way. The influence on the choice of materials—white stone and brick—was drawn from a few hundred yards away, Dulwich College. The Great Hall, built in the mid-nineteeth century and designed by Charles Barry Jr, is made of complex and ornate brickwork, adorned with complex stone-string courses, finials, parapets and gable ends. Later in the 1960s the new Christison Hall was built; designed by Manfred Bresgens and Malcolm Pringle of Austin Vernon and Partners, it provides a modern take on decorated brickwork. These two buildings were built in different eras but both celebrate and play with the possibilities of brickwork and became the inspiration for the playful brickwork at College Road.

"The garden comes into the house in the guest bedroom with its door out into the garden and its glass corner, and the bathroom is beautifully top-lit."

— **Tom Wells**

1 Kitchen
2 Dining
3 Living
4 Bedroom
5 Study
6 Utility
7 Shower/Bathroom
8 Plant/Store

Responding to orientation, the undulating north wall is constructed from header bricks with few perforations making a smooth, curving, castle-like construction facing the flat north light. The garden elevation facing south has a smooth, simple stretcher bond at garden level but above, in panels between the bay windows, saw tooth brickwork provides a three-dimensional quality. The pattern gives varying shadow and light as it runs around the curved east end of the house. The client said "the brickwork feels part of the garden, solid, like the prow of a ship".

The brickwork was drawn and constructed with care. Exacting drawings setting out precisely every line and curve provided the builders with a challenge, taken up with relish by a top-quality team of bricklayers. As the walls grew up from the scaffolding they stood back and took photos on their phones. We were told that they were so pleased with their work that these photos were shown round the pub on Friday night with pride. For us, this is what building should be about, a project for everyone involved: making work to be proud of where every element of material craftsmanship and detail becomes an essential part of the picture, where even a brick can be something.

Of course everything was not always perfect though and two particular incidents spring to mind. The slates on the apse end of the curving slate roof were laid badly and appeared faceted, not smooth as we had envisaged. After much sucking of teeth and debate about what was and was not possible, we took a photo of a Victorian church in nearby Goose Green with a beautiful, curving, pitched slate roof: "If they could do it then you can do it now. The materials and construction methods are the same." To their credit, the roofers took up the baton, the slates came off and went back on again, this time worthy of a Victorian craftsman.

The other incident involved the special doorbell, a stone face. This arrived on site supposedly made to our drawing but with very poorly finished edges and detail. Sometimes with special, nonstandard items we just have to roll up our sleeves and be proactive. At the time we were also working on a Grade II-listed building in Somerset, just outside Bath, and on site, making replacement fireplaces and repairing original stone details, was a woman stonemason, Hailey Diamond. Helpful and interested in her craft, she took the poorly finished stone home and finished it beautifully, returning it the following week for us to collect and deliver back to the site in London.

top construction photo—stonemason at work on the letter box (see p 128).

bottom east elevation.

opposite detail of curved saw tooth brickwork on apse.

opposite detail of front gable.

top view of bathroom turrets and lanterns at dusk.

bottom view of bathroom turrets and lanterns during the day.

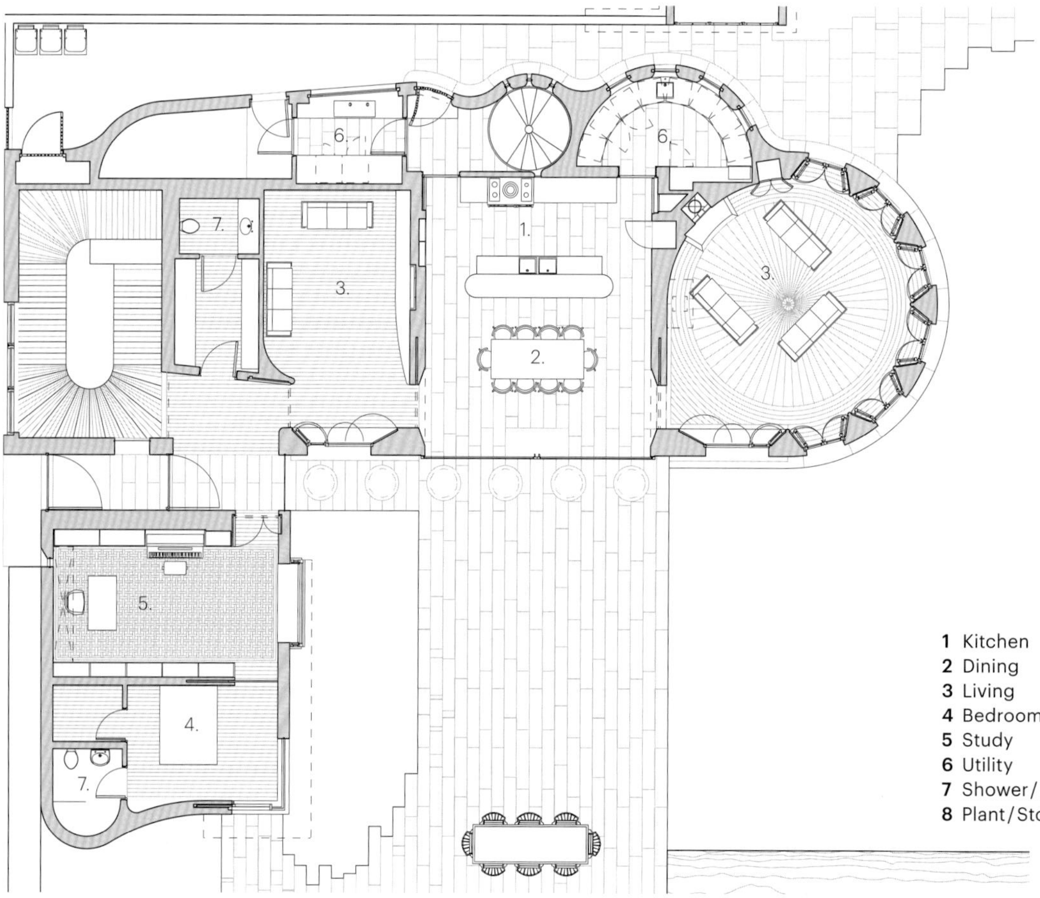

1 Kitchen
2 Dining
3 Living
4 Bedroom
5 Study
6 Utility
7 Shower/Bathroom
8 Plant/Store

Overall this was a project where, time after time, real quality craftsmen stepped up and showed us what they could do. The French polisher, a Chelsea fan, full of banter and bravado, took huge pride in what he did; creating glass-like finishes to handrails, perfectly smooth to the touch. The project was lucky as, in the recurring theme throughout this book, it is ultimately individuals who make the difference. Here it was Graham Frost, the site agent, who pulled it all together. This was his final job before retiring. He had worked in construction since he was 15 and had much to teach everyone: a beady eye, great clarity and common sense. He was determined that he would go out on a high.

Seven years on, does the house live up to the dreams and aspirations of the client? We asked them to just tell us how they feel about the house, no holding back. It was heartening to hear that they positively enjoyed designing and building the house with us and that "they never felt tense about the process". They talked about how calming the house is and the positive effect they feel it has had on their girls growing up. Their favourite room is the circular sitting room, "the prow of the ship" where they can get away from the hubbub and feel entirely connected to the garden: "it is a heavenly calm space which transforms at Christmas and in summer it becomes part of the garden. It has a spirit in every season." Predictably, the kitchen is where "everyone lives". Interestingly for us, one of the things that makes the difference here is the way "the relationship of the larder to kitchen to dining to garden works perfectly".

"The circular sitting room... is a heavenly calm space which transforms at Christmas and in summer it becomes part of the garden."

— **Tom Wells**

opposite top sitting room timber floor.

opposite bottom ground floor plan.

left construction photos—painstakingly creating the radiating timber floor.

right detail of central flower in floor.

39

opposite detail of doorbell, camera, speaker and letter box.

above detail of timber window on gable-facing road.

We were heartened to hear that our special details and intention to give spaces and places certain characters had been noticed and enjoyed. "The doors which disappear into reveals are perfect, allowing flexibility of space... especially for the TV room and girls' bedrooms", and the way "the pitch of roof in the bedrooms makes you feel you are under a sail". They mentioned in particular the splayed reveals, lined with mirror, to the doors connecting the principal ground floor living spaces, creating intriguing reflections. They love seeing the garden in them, "you get a completely different view from the next person".

This is a house with two staircases and we wanted to know how their two very different characters had worked in practice. Whilst talking about the grand front stair facing the road, the client mentioned that they would like help with finding something dramatic to decorate the main wall facing the road: What did we think? We agreed that a dramatic work hung facing out is what it needs, so the search is on.

left view from kitchen to front stair.

right first floor landing.

opposite front, main stair.

overleaf detail of rooflight over turret stair.

The front staircase is visible from the street through mullions which get closer together as they travel down to ground level to achieve some privacy. This stair is less frequently used on an everyday basis, but this does not bother the client, who loves its drama and the buffer it creates to the street. There is a real issue relating to living in a special house in that people feel they can approach and peer in, in a way that they would not dream of doing otherwise. Because of this, we designed a mirrored shutter for the little lookout window into the study, so that you can look out when you want to but can close it from inquisitive eyes otherwise (see p 128).

"The doors which disappear into reveals are perfect, allowing flexibility of space [and the way] the pitch of roof in the bedrooms makes you feel you are under a sail."

— **Tom Wells**

For the second turret stair, set into the brick castle wall, we used expertise developed working with aluminium casting on a previous project in the Channel Islands. Three storeys of stairs gives just enough repetition to make casting of repeated elements viable. Working with the casting foundry, we developed a simple repeated bracket casting to support each oak tread. We then specified a polished finish to catch the light. The final stair is "a tour de force, it is a castle-shaped piece of sculpture—we love it and it is used continually". Its secrecy and jewel-like details make it special, and our clients' clear appreciation of it makes it worth the effort.

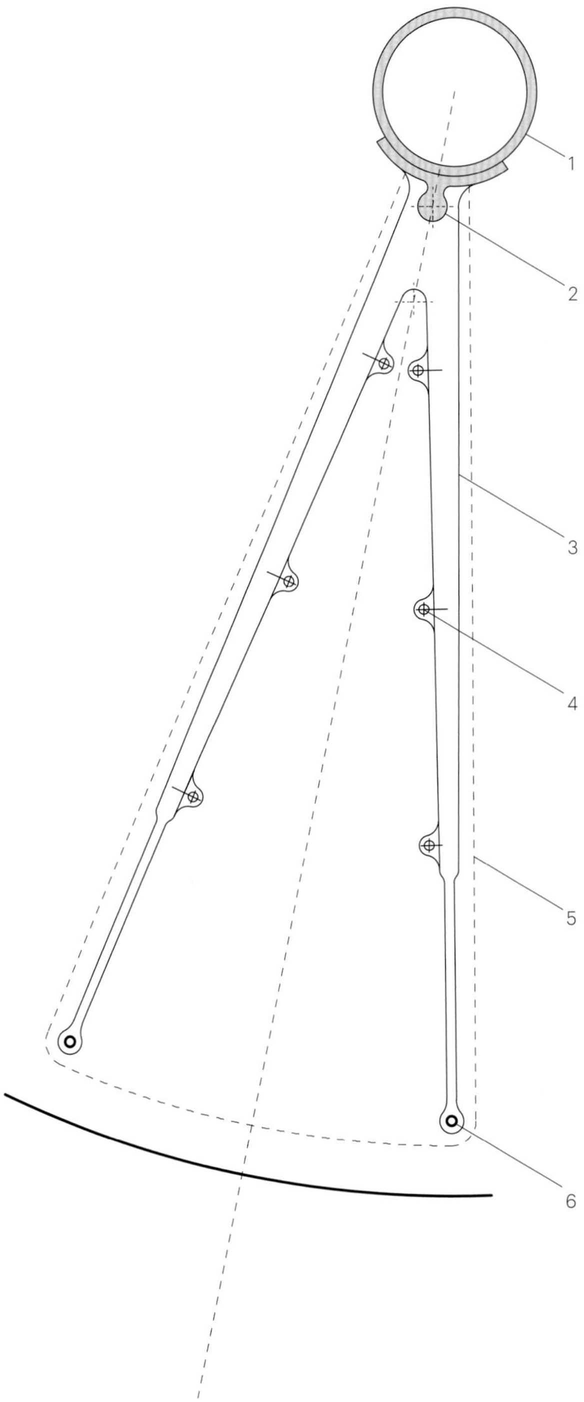

1 168.3 mm od CHS with 10 mm wall
2 Circular aluminium peg level with top face of timber
3 Aluminium chassis
4 6 mm thick tang with countersunk hole for No10 woodscrew
5 Quarter-sawn English oak tread
6 10 mm dia countersunk hole for M10 bolt

right detail of cast aluminium wishbone.

opposite turret stair.

opposite the front door from the hall.

below timber reading bays facing the garden.

overleaf view at dusk of front elevation gable.

Finally we wanted to know what was the most unexpected surprise in the house, good or bad? "The front door, everyone we meet says: 'Are you the ones with the coloured front door, I love it.' At night it glows and during the day the afternoon sun throws colours onto the wall inside. We deliberated about it at the time but it is a winner." This explained a phone call we received in the studio, from someone asking where we got the door, who made it and how could they get one for their house?

We take time to give careful thought to every junction, move and decision, drawing and testing and drawing again to get it right, and endorse wholeheartedly David Chipperfield's remark that "The difference between good and bad architecture is the time you spend on it".

It was reassuring to hear that the energy and effort expended was worth it, when our client said (of the benefits of good design): "We take for granted things others don't even know they have missed."

"At night it glows and during the day the afternoon sun throws colours onto the wall inside."

— **Tom Wells**

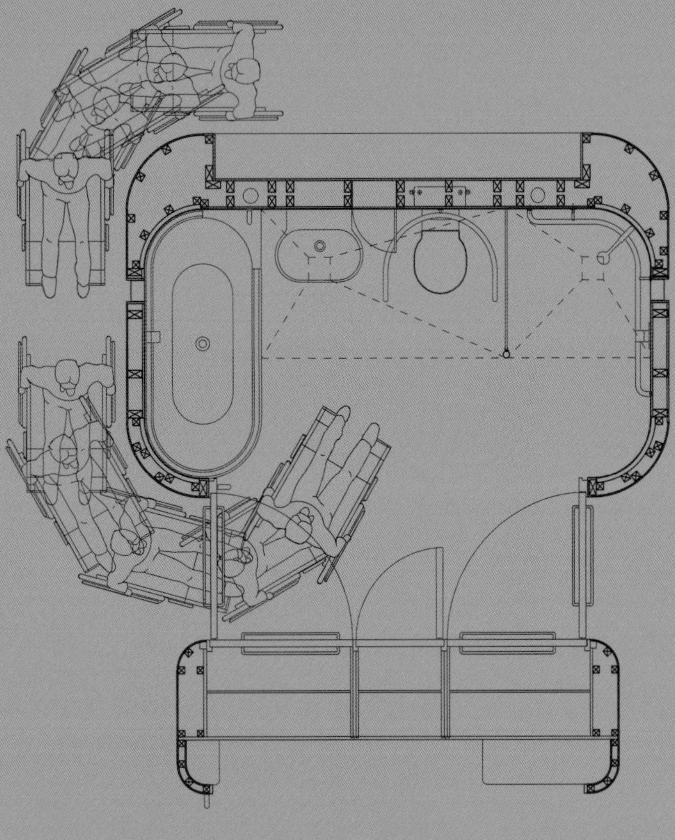

Chapter seven

"A Poetic Exercise in Wood" — Kevin McCloud

Holly Barn

Norfolk Broads, 2005

Alan and Jenny Rogers had a small cottage in Reedham, Norfolk. They loved the village but wanted something bigger, something that could comfortably accommodate Alan as his rheumatoid arthritis progressed. They had just had their apartment in London renovated by Mary-Lou Arscott, who worked with us until she left for Pittsburgh in 2006. They asked Mary-Lou and through her, us, to build them a new house on the Norfolk Broads. In 2004 they bought an old barn on half a site, the other half of which the farmer committed to sell to them the following year.

There were bats in the old barn and the planners were clear that only a building of a similar size and form sitting on the same footprint would be acceptable. We knew we were to build a new Holly Barn. Alan and Jenny were keen to get started so a design was developed quickly and by the autumn of 2004 we were talking to a local builder Alan trusted and knew well: Gary Hayes of Willow Builders. Alan had mentioned Gary to us as being someone he wanted to work with to make up for a previous failed project. This made us a little anxious. Planning permission was granted in early in 2005, by which time conversations with Gary were well underway.

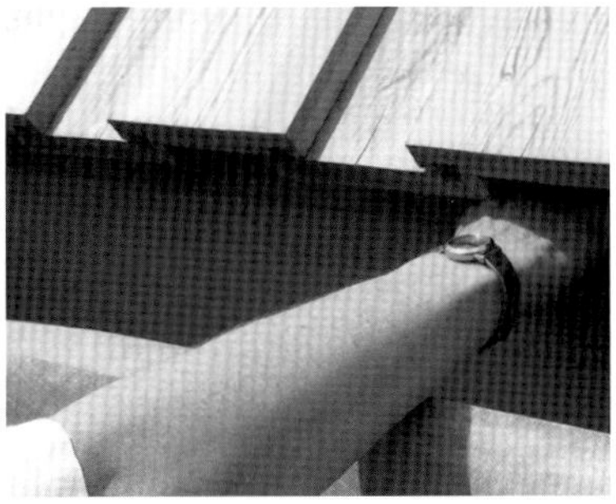

The planners had prescribed the barn form and we were happy to work with it and explore how to use timber in a contemporary way. Timber resonated with the boathouses along the river and the windmills of the Broads. We developed a sophisticated cladding system of Siberian larch-banded wide and narrow boards. This variation helped coordinate the boards with windows and doors, allowing for some adjustment. We would never chop into a board, although we did make deliberate holes as access to bat boxes behind the cladding and for mechanical ventilation. We wanted the barn to have a smooth skin, reminiscent of an upturned hull, so we concealed the gutters. Although a little risky, we abandoned traditional gutters and made recessed gutters lined with fibreglass instead. This achieved exactly the form we wanted and they have stood up well. We wanted to make a timber roof but were nervous about its performance over time. The exact detail, based on the principle that the natural cupping of a plank should be exploited by laying concave under and convex over, was developed and researched extensively with Patrick Hislop at TRADA.

The barn itself has a steel frame. We wanted this to be simple and agricultural to reflect the building type and location. Even so, it was demanding to draw and detail. We checked and coordinated every member and connection on the fabrication drawings. Willow Builders came from the other side of the water so all the building materials were brought across by ferry.

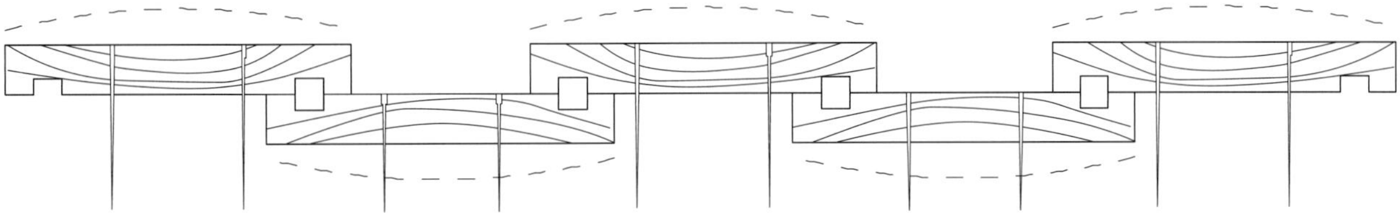

opposite view of the entrance gable with Reedham Church beyond.

top and middle construction photos—the steel frame going up and the timber roof planks at the eaves.

bottom detail showing timber roof planks laid to take advantage of their natural cupping.

30

The decision to put the main living spaces upstairs and the bedrooms downstairs (with the exception of Alan and Jenny's) was an early one. From this first floor piano nobile, panoramic views across the Broads were possible. The windows were continuous linear bands just below the eaves, low enough to be viewed from a wheelchair and with an Arts and Craft curved plaster detail dropping from the ceiling down to the low eaves and tops of windows, which slide open completely. A glass balustrade becomes the only barrier to the outside, making the room feel as though it is a veranda or semi-outdoor space.

The first floor benefited from the full volume of the roof. With no specific dedicated circulation space, this floor became a single large volume divided by eaves-height walls topped with glass hung from the ceiling and supported on the walls to give acoustic separation, just as we had done at New Maltings a few years earlier. The plan is simple, with the hall at one end and Alan and Jenny's bedroom at the other, with its own pod bathroom. Between these ends are the main living spaces, with a low windowsill running the entire length.

On the ground floor is a line of monastic cell bedrooms with private windows looking out of the back of the barn, whilst along the front are a double line of doors with a cloister-like space between and double doors opening out onto the garden. Curved edges feature here and upstairs, allowing easy movement of a wheelchair, no bumping and bashing into corners, as well as being an attractive feature. Between the bedrooms and the hall is a games room where Alan and his adult sons can play pool late into the night without disturbing Jenny.

"Alan didn't see the first floor until the lift was commissioned at the end of the job. He was overwhelmed."

— Gary Hayes, Willow Builders Ltd

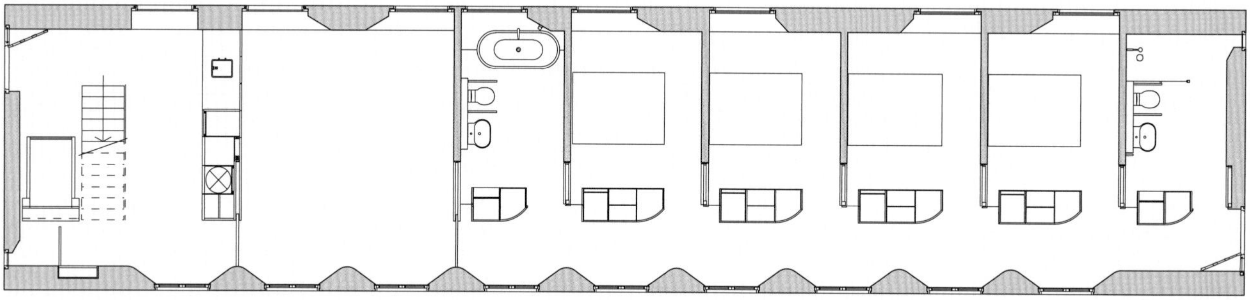

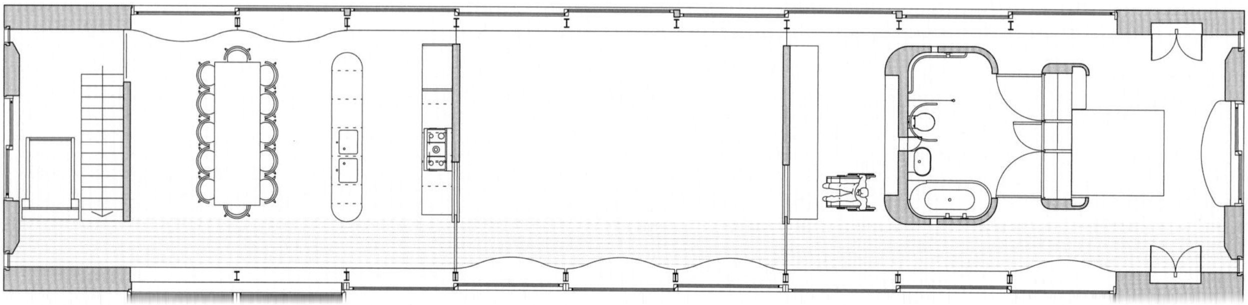

pp 144–145 view of Holly Barn from the reed beds.

pp 146–147 detail of timber cladding and sliding windows.

opposite top detail showing curved plaster soffit to windows.

opposite bottom ground and first floor plans.

top plans showing wheelchair routes round curved walls.

bottom view of bedroom corridor.

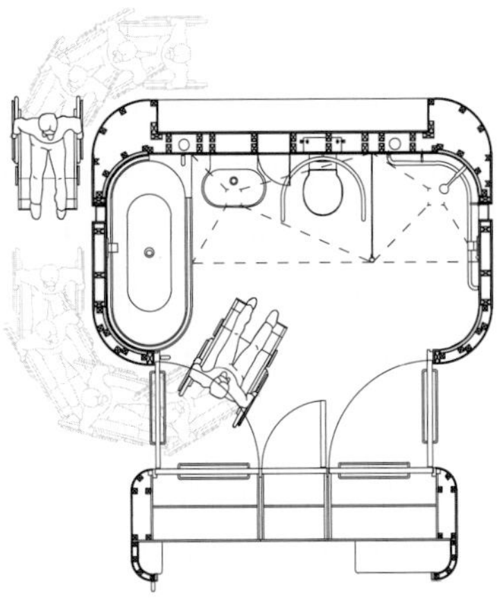

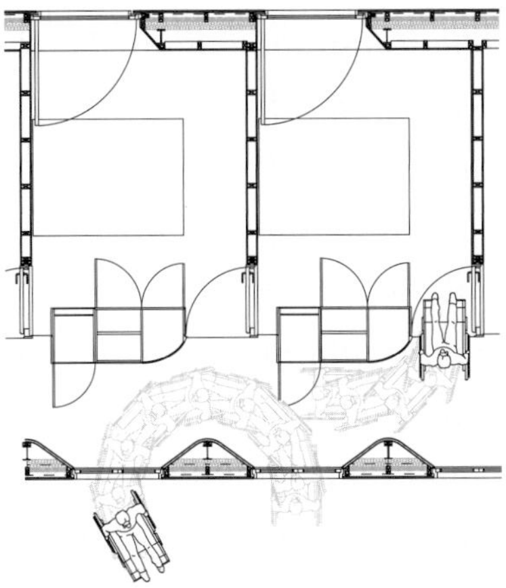

left construction photos—forming the curved plastered eaves and installing the slatted gable end.

right view of kitchen looking down the full length of the barn.

Finally, there is a lift in the hall to take a wheelchair up to the main living floor. The lift was the last thing to be installed, and until it was, Alan in his wheelchair could not get up to see the first floor. The day came and Alan ascended the lift. Gary reminded us that "Alan didn't see the first floor until the lift was commissioned at the end of the job. He was overwhelmed." Alan talked about the wonder of the space and how he had doubted that he might ever see it. He loved Holly Barn and later told us that sitting at his desk upstairs looking out over the Broads he often forgot he was disabled; for us the greatest compliment possible.

The building is made from relatively cheap materials and the finishes inside are not expensive. When we met Gary he was used to working to a budget and had been building brick care homes, which he jokingly told us he "built to the nearest brick". Looking back he says he thought it was a "realistic budget. I always prefer to negotiate a project to get the best value." He has found recently that clients "question everything, and are not so willing to accept what is drawn. I know it is a big leap of faith but everyone needs to be on board for the philosophy of the build." Gary's comments on what he finds helpful on a project are illuminating:

> Builders give their best if there is a personal challenge. Holly Barn's information was overwhelming at the beginning. The quality of the drawings is important… [the] drawings were very good but it was [helpful] to have them talked through so that I can understand what are the most important details. Three-dimensional models are very useful for everyone to understand the building. Remember, 75 per cent of the building industry is dyslexic!

Holly Barn brought Gary much success and he has gone on to build two more Manser Medal winners but he says that "Holly Barn was my most enjoyable project, and I look back on it as fond times."

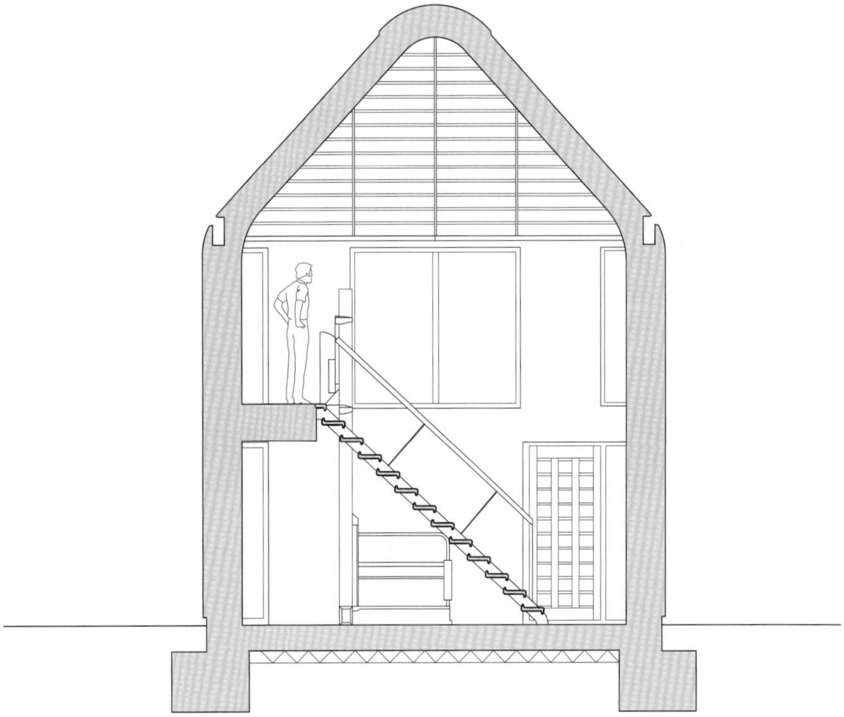

opposite detail of stair.

left detail of timber cladding windows and corner.

right cross section.

overleaf Holly Barn at dusk.

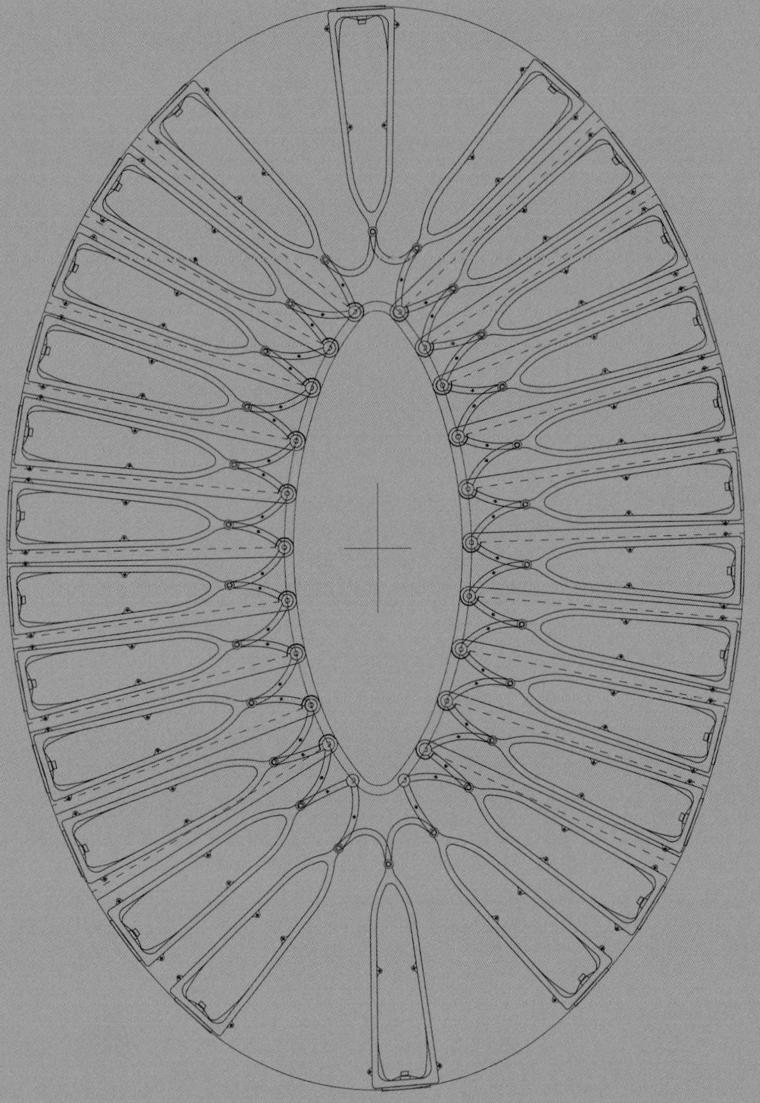

Chapter eight

Making of a Stair
Tudor House
Guernsey, 2003

Making of a Stair

> As an architect, you cannot be so arrogant as to say you are 100 per cent sure about what you do. A builder is like a little god—somebody who does things, doesn't just draw things.
>
> — **Renzo Piano**

When you design something complex and exacting make sure you are confident that if no one else can, you understand how and are able to build it. This is the story of the making of a stair in a mixed-use building in St Peter Port, Guernsey. The project was a large mixed-use development we completed in 2003, which explored and used cast aluminium extensively, and went on to be joint winner of the 2003 Aluminium Imagination Award, recognised specifically for its innovative and imaginative use of aluminium. The material was used primarily for the facade and grand stair. The project was described at the time by the Award Judge Ian Richie as "dripping with aluminium".

The stair in question is a helical staircase with a cast aluminium structure, which formed the focal point of a four-storey building of office accommodation. The staircase measures 3.2 x 4.4 m, and spirals through four storeys under an elliptical rooflight. It is constructed using individual cast aluminium 'wishbones' linked together to form a continuous helix. The stair structure works in much the same way as a traditional stone cantilever staircase, each individual tread taking support from the step above and below it, with the whole staircase acting as a single continuous structure, further reinforced by the helical handrail above.

The staircase is divided between a hidden structure (wall fixings behind the face of the plaster) and a structure that can be seen. The structure was manufactured using LM6 cast aluminium, cast in sand and given a bead blasted finish. The treads are maple, each supported on a 900 mm long wishbone fork. 200 mm long 'V' fingers are connected to the end of the wishbone casting. This is a pin joint so it can pivot either side for adjustment, and to link onto the adjacent tread's finger via cylindrical blocking pieces. This connection onto the adjoining finger above and below provides the strength to the helix. A variety of 'finger' castings can be fitted to the end of the wishbone chassis to support half and full landings. A single bolt locks tapered aluminium balusters to the top of the 'V' fingers. A universal joint at the top of the tapered balusters enables tolerance for fixing the helical aluminium circular handrail. The handrail forms a helical truss, which further braces the staircase.

The wishbone chassis are supported by first fix cast aluminium housing brackets (measuring 100 x 200 x 50 mm) bolted to the curved brick wall. The housing bracket comprised of two components: a semi spherical 'socket' box, and a plate with a semi spherical 'ball' for fitting into the socket on the box. This 'ball and socket' joint gives the wishbone all round adjustment: to the left or right and up or down. The body of the aluminium box is lost behind the face of the plaster. The face of the ball plate and the housing bracket determined the face of the plaster wall. A single central M18 bolt locked the wishbone fork to the first fix housing bracket.

opposite top left ball socket wall fixing for wishbone chassis.

opposite middle left detail of tread and balustrade components—working together structurally.

opposite bottom left completed stair against polished plaster wall.

opposite right 3D drawing showing elliptical spiral of stair.

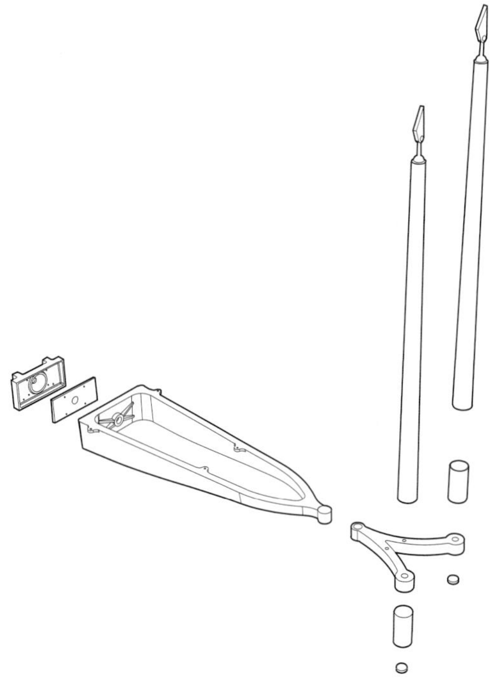

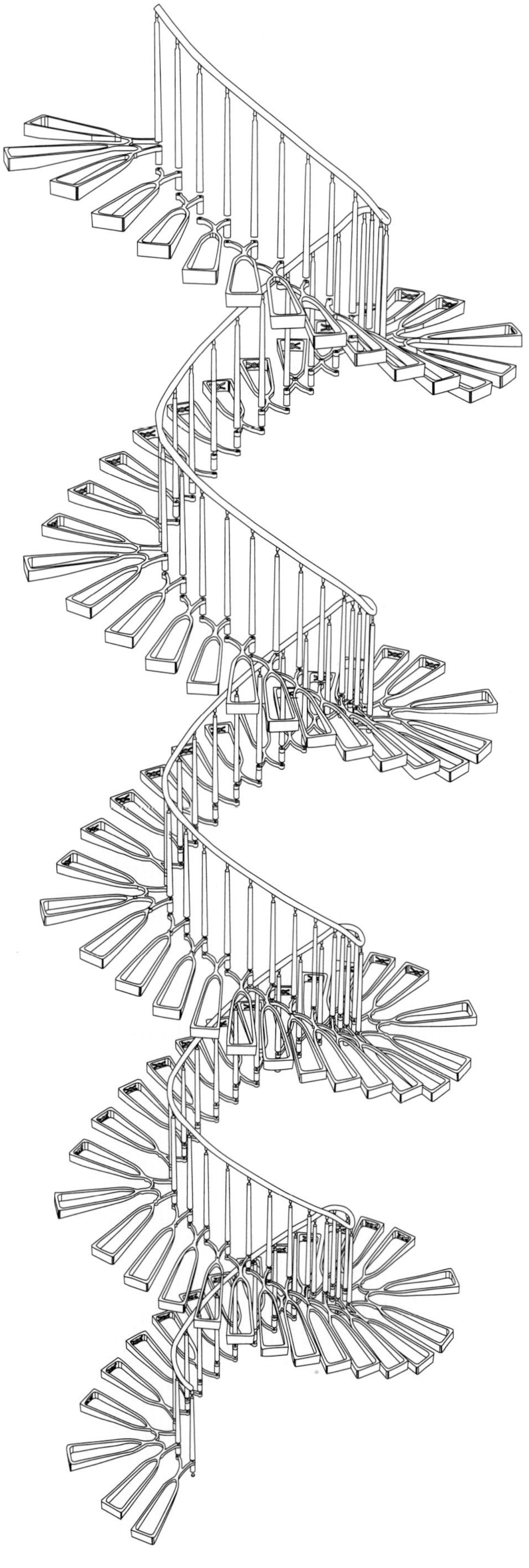

left construction photos, setting out the stair.

right looking up at wishbone construction from below.

opposite looking down on stair maple treads.

If this all sounds exacting and complex, it was, and in practice the contractor was completely perplexed and had no confidence that he would be able to construct it. This was not helped by the fact that the subcontractor supplying and fixing the staircase structure had fabricated a jig to assist with setting out the first fix aluminium housing brackets, which proved to be inaccurate, and could not be relied upon.

Convinced that it would not work, they asked us to come out to Guernsey and assist with the set out of their first fix wall fixings. Simon took the next plane to Guernsey. He reviewed the work of the subcontractor and responded robustly to their premise that it was impossible to build. He decided to establish the set out of the middle fixing on the first half landing. This would minimise any dimensional 'creep' with the overall set out. This middle fixing was established by triangulating from the central axis of the elliptical stair. Once this fixing had been established, the wall fixings could be made up and down the first flight. When each of the first flight fixings had been established, the others followed more easily and were set out by plumb line and measurement taken from the first. Breaking new ground with unfamiliar materials for the contractor created unpredictable tensions and anxiety, however we eventually formed an effective team with the subcontractor and finished the staircase.

"A builder is like a little god—somebody who does things, doesn't just draw things."

— **Renzo Piano**

opposite looking up through half landings to rooflight above.

below drawings showing stair and cast aluminium components in plan.

The finished stair has an unexpected organic quality. The wishbone soffit of the stair has been likened to being in a dinosaur's rib cage, an interlinking piece of jewellery, and even Gothic perpendicular vaulting. The intricacy and three-dimensional structural quality of the originally imagined concept has been realised through careful, detailed and accurate drawings, and a real working understanding of sequencing and tolerance of a complex building process to produce a powerful result. Peter Zumthor recognises this interdependence, "What I try to do is the art of building, and the art of building is the art of construction; it is not only about forms and shapes and images."

"What I try to do is the art of building, and the art of building is the art of construction; it is not only about forms and shapes and images."

— **Peter Zumthor**

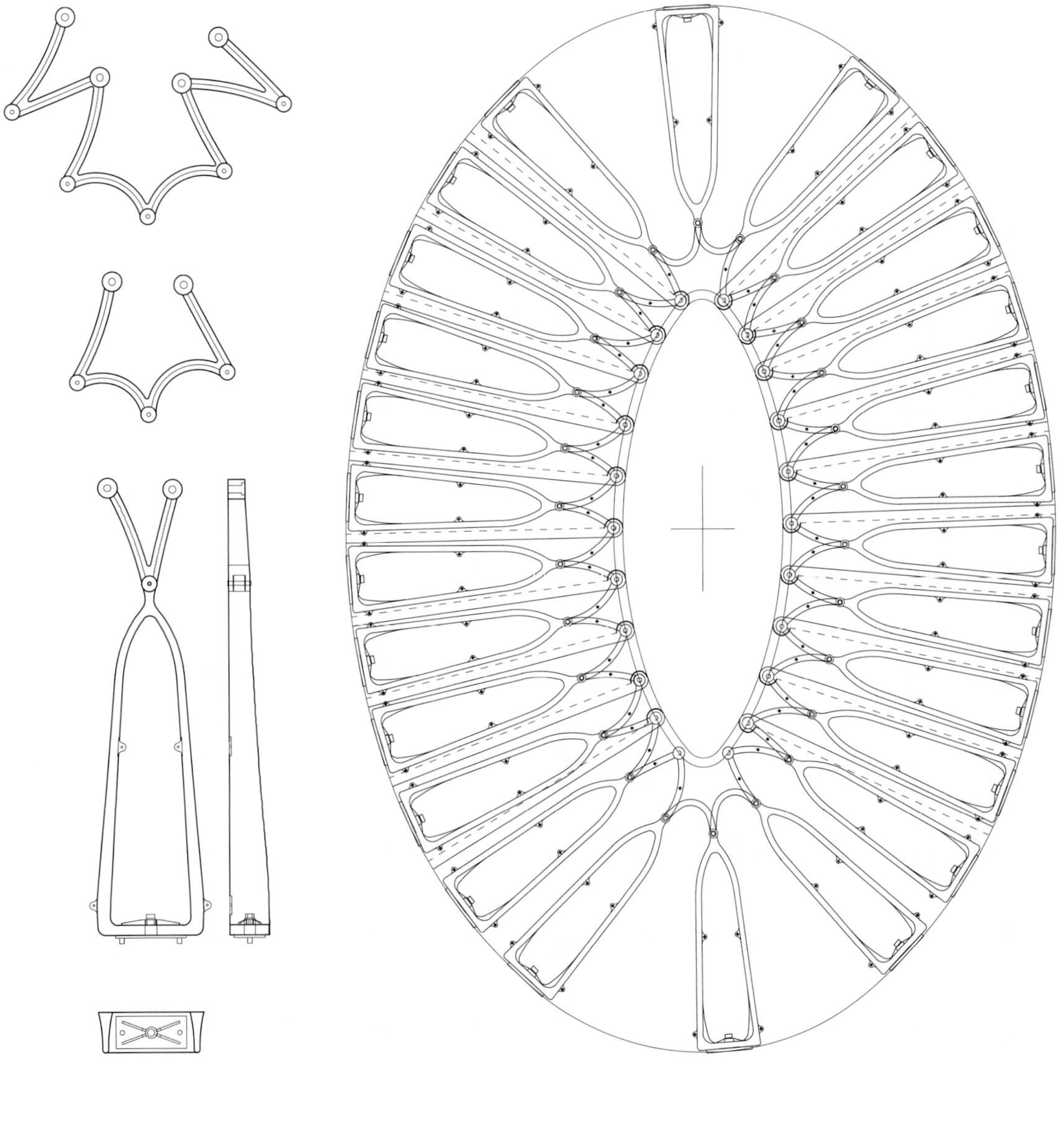

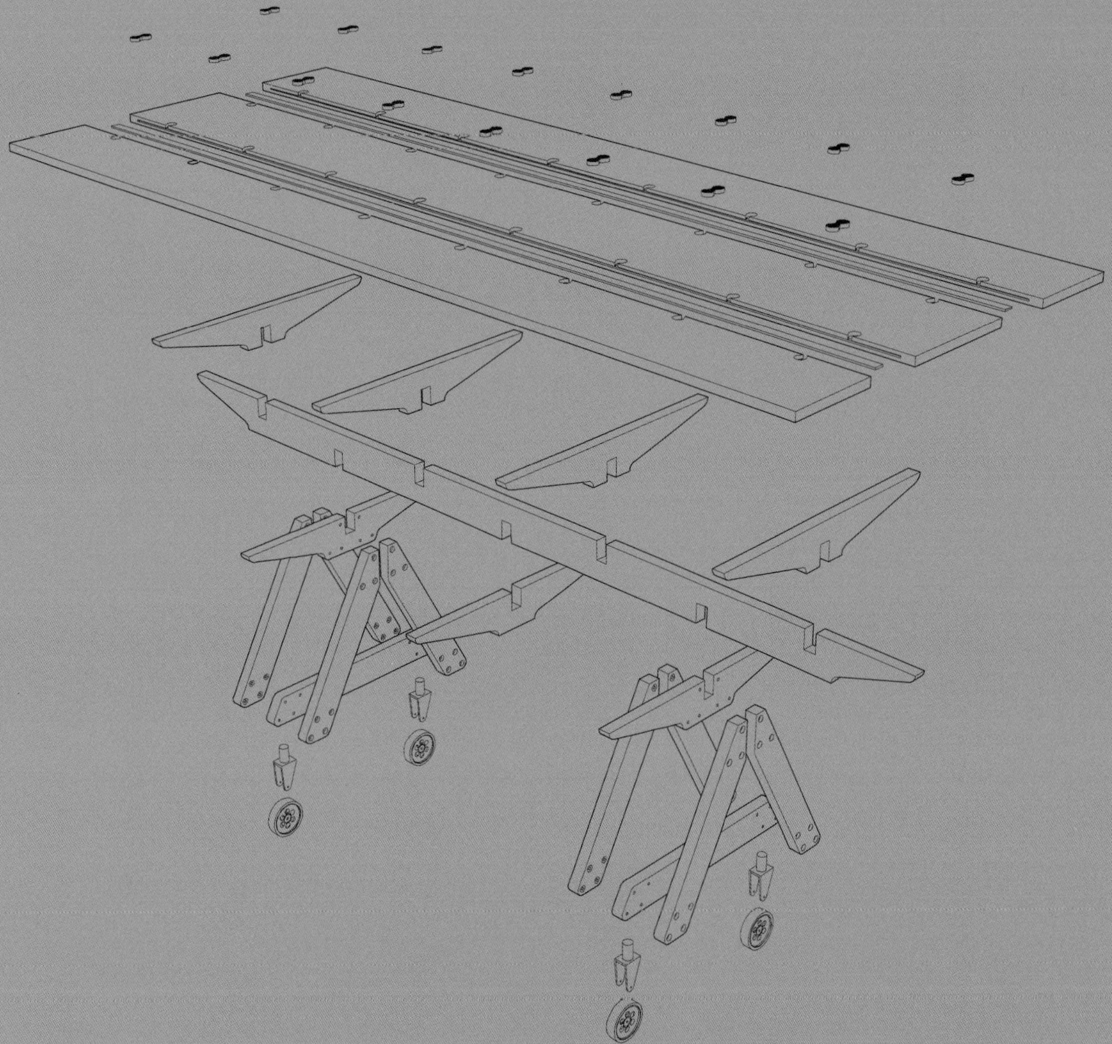

Chapter nine

Four Tables, No Legs

Table

London, 1995–2015

Four Tables, No Legs

In 1995 we were on a visit to see Simon Smith at WL West and Sons in West Sussex to select timber for a project. Simon has helped us source specialist timber for over 20 years. Knowing how we appreciate his wood, he beckoned us over to look at three majestic, wide English oak planks, all from the same tree. Seduced by their beauty we bought them, without knowing what we could we do with them. Later, looking at the width and grain of the planks, a table seemed the obvious answer.

Looking at our three planks we could see that set side by side, with the widest 360 mm plank straddled by the two narrower 260 mm planks, all screwed and pelleted onto a chassis, they would make a perfect robust table top for outside. The 3 m oiled planks would weather to compliment our York stone garden terrace, which surrounded by pleached hornbeams makes a perfect outside dining room.

The table needed to be manoeuvrable and flexible, able to fit many small children along a bench on one side and adults in comfortable chairs along the other. We designed a ribbed chassis supported by two triangles, one at either end. The chassis sat on the top of the triangle with galvanised swivel wheels on the other two corners, enabling the table to be wheeled easily in any direction. This triangular support, made from a solid square section of timber from the same tree, allowed for flexibility in a way that a conventional leg at each corner could not. When crowded or with just a few people there was no uncomfortable bashing of knees under the table. The chassis made our planks appear to hover, a horizontal, rectangular, floating timber plane, growing old gracefully and looking better and better with the patina that comes from many years of use.

"The chassis made our planks appear to hover, a horizontal, rectangular, floating timber plane, growing old gracefully."

left reviewing a work experience student's project in the garden.

right Celia and Hugo playing chess on the table at Hodges Place.

opposite our first table in the garden outside the office.

above the most recent table with bog oak black butterfly joints.

opposite left Christmas dinner at Hodges Place.

opposite right the most recent table hung with three-legged Wegner chairs.

overleaf detail showing triangular chassis.

Five years after making the first table, we designed a second specifically for the dining and living space at Hodges Place. This time it would be kept inside. The brief was to seat up to 20 people. Maeve (the owner) said, "I am very fond of the table. This morning I had breakfast on it alone, looking across the pond, but we have actually squashed 25 people around it as well."

To meet the brief this table needed to be 1 m longer than the first. This time we made it from American oak, which is blonder and straighter grained than English oak. We also made two matching oak benches, one for each side, which fit snugly between the supporting triangles. In this version, the original galvanised wheels became smart yellow and chrome. Maeve said that, "I love the way the benches tuck underneath or spread along the wall.... It's very easy to move around which means it is moved around quite regularly—even your aged mother can manage it." Although the oiled oak would, over the years, become a little darker from the sunlight it would never gather the weathered patina of the original outdoor prototype. The table was designed for a specific room: "Not everyone is lucky enough to have a bespoke table. The table must stay in the room I can't imagine it without it. It is part of the room, and if I ever have to leave, the table must stay in this room."

More versions of the table were then commissioned by friends and clients, each customised to suit their circumstances. One 4 m version, commissioned by a friend, was made by a shipwright familiar with the ribbed chassis construction. Instead of finishing the timber with oil as the others had been, he varnished it with a high-gloss, boat finish.

"We love this elegant table which is brilliantly adaptable for just the two of us or larger groups. It gets used for everything and I sometimes think our lives sit on it!"

— **Helen Boaden**

opposite Hodges Place table with its matching benches.

below plan, section, elevations and component pieces.

Then eight years later, in 2013, a smart and compact apartment in Notting Hill needed a table for its long but narrow kitchen. This time the table was smaller, only 0.7 m wide and 1.8 m long. It was made of ash with a milk white base stain covered by a clear lacquer. Rollers replaced the swivel casters, because of the constricted space. These allowed the table to be pulled in and out to give easy access to a long upholstered banquet seat, but stopped it from roaming and rolling around in all directions within a smaller space, which works well for this client. "We love this elegant table which is brilliantly adaptable for just the two of us or larger groups. It gets used for everything and I sometimes think our lives sit on it!"

Finally we decided to design an indoor / kitchen version of the table for ourselves. This would mirror our old friend, now 21 years old, dark and a little warped from sitting outside in all weathers. Because we were designing it for ourselves, this new table created an opportunity to experiment and develop the design further. This time it would be 3 m long and be a completely flat pack, dry constructed table. We wanted to express the construction as decoration. We called it our "flat pack table". Made of English oak like the first table, the planks were connected using bog-oak expressed butterfly fixings to decorate the surface, a detail we like using because it expresses the construction, like a dovetailed joint both practical and decorative.

"I love the way the benches tuck underneath or spread along the wall.... It's very easy to move around which means it is moved around quite regularly."
— **Maeve Bhavan**

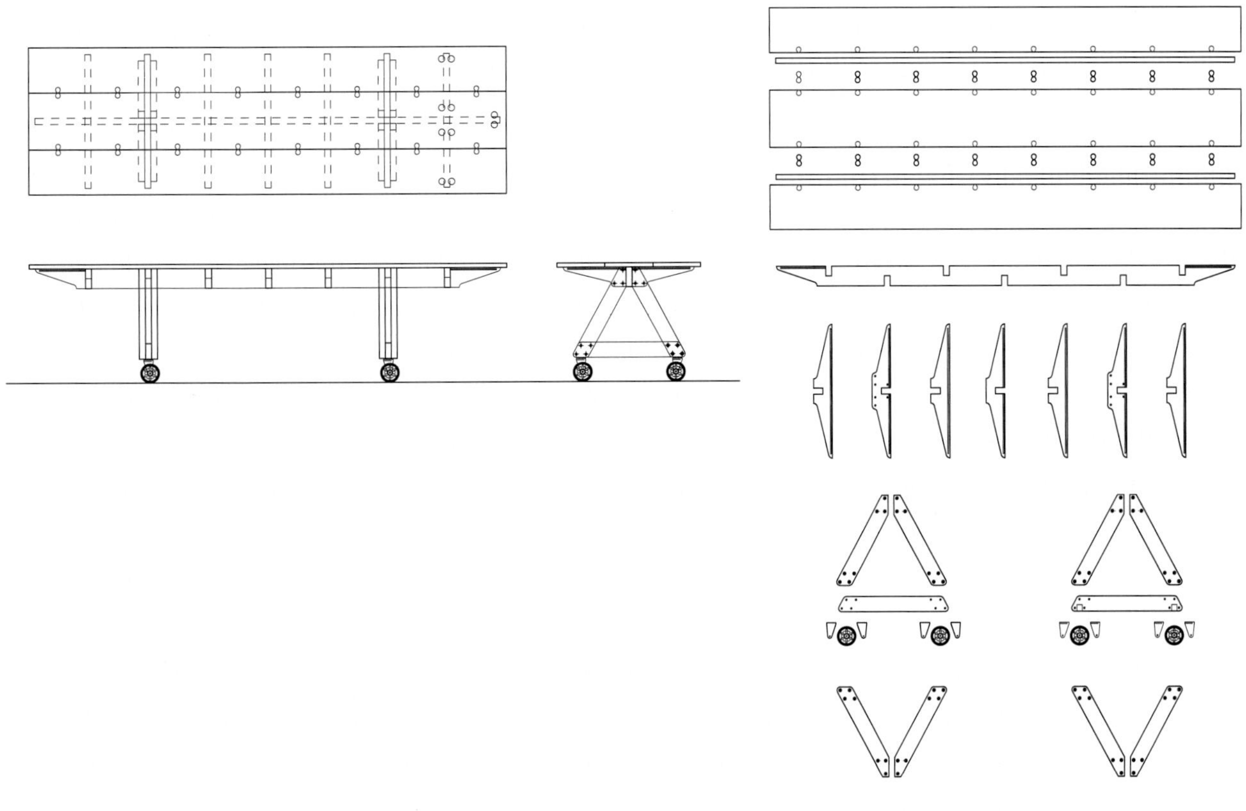

The chassis is dry assembled to create a spine with projecting ribs. Unlike the previous tables the two supporting triangles were also designed to be dry assembled from plank offcuts. So instead of being a single solid section of timber it was fabricated from pairs of planks bolted together at the three points of the triangle. This meant all the timber for the table could come from the same tree. Wheelchair wheels were used in place of the casters for all-round manoeuvrability.

Joiner Aaron Brown made this table for us. Looking back he says, "I thought the design of the table was so nice. It was entirely apparent how the assembly was thought through as were the component parts. It really appealed to me. I understood the tension between aesthetic and strategy. There is a nice balance between functionality, efficiency and aesthetic." Pleased to be asked to make the table, he said, "individual pieces are a pleasure to do", but commented that if asked to build the table again he would ask for the timber to be supplied unmilled. We initially specified the final finish on the advice of a floor restorer we were working with. Aaron was sceptical but applied the finish saying, "I would have used Danish Oil." He had the last word because as he predicted it was a nightmare, showing every oil and water mark so Aaron came back with his Danish Oil, sanded and finished the table again, this time for good.

When you touch and use a piece of furniture, whether it is a twelfth-century refectory table or a mid-century modern chair, it becomes part of life, improves with age and gives great pleasure in use. Every version of this table has been touched and wiped down, laden with food, paper, homework, shopping and laptops, combining the everyday with the aesthetic. They become part of the lives of their owners as they transform from pristine new objects into worn and weathered witnesses to the lives lived over them. As Charles Eames said, "Eventually everything connects—people, ideas, objects. The quality of the connections is the key to quality per se."

"I thought the design of the table was so nice. It was entirely apparent how the assembly was thought through as were the component parts, it really appealed to me. I understood the tension between aesthetic and strategy. There is a nice balance between functionality, efficiency and aesthetic."

— **Aaron Brown, Joiner**

above detail of the bog oak butterfly connection.

opposite exploded isometric of the table.

overleaf view of underside of table showing full chassis support system.

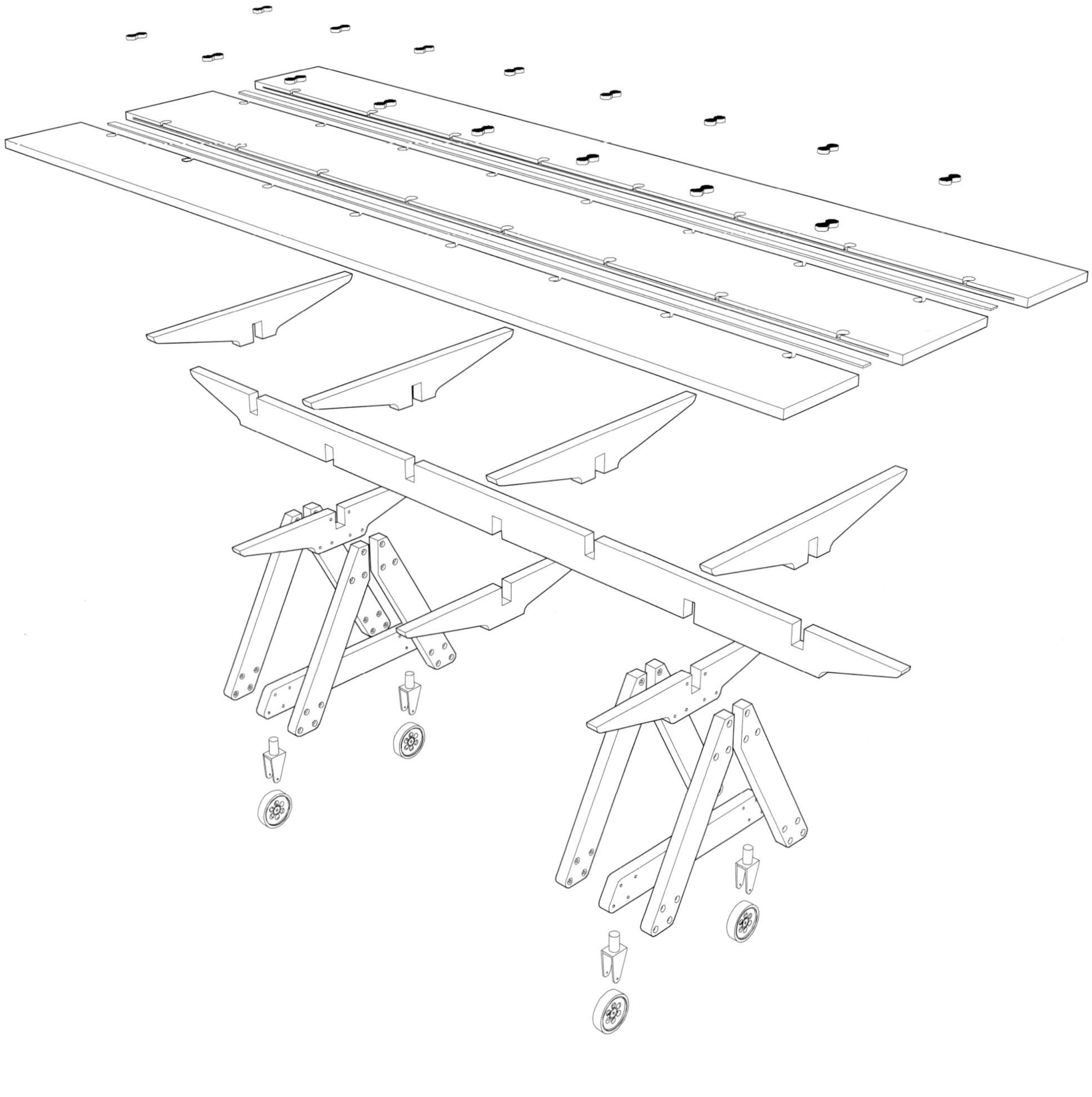

Epilogue

People Present and Past
Bushey Hill Studio
London, 1995–2016

People Present and Past

Sasha Bhavan
Simon Knox
Katherine Johnson
Ana Abascal
Lydia Stott
Evelyn Ting
Emily Glazier
Ben Hair
Fergus Knox

Mary-Lou Arscott	1996–2006
Alex Austin	2000–2001
Louise Potter	2001–2003
Tina Wilson	2000–2001
Tracy Reid	2001
Barry Mitchell	2002–2003
Mark Tinker	2002
Dominic Hailey	2002
Peter Kirkham	2002
James Foster	2003
Mark Stokes	2004
Sarah Evans	2004
Tim Dunseath	2004
Lucy Thomas	2004–2015
Jeremy Joseph	2003–2006
James Gardener	2006
Elinor Line	2007–2011
Ronan Watts	2007
Tim Phillips	2007–2008
Brad Pickard	2008
Jan Balbaligo	2008–2012
Katarzyna Dobosz	2008–2009
Ben Ridley	2010–2011
Marcus Aitman	2009
Magda Gawlik	2010–2011
Méabh McCarthy	2011–2013
Andrew MacMurray	2014–2015
Nick Woodford	2014–2015
Jack Leather	2015
Marianna Fillipou	2015
Celia Knox	2015

previous page Bushey Hill Studio.

opposite *Needle Fish,* Thomas Hill, Bushey Hill Studio.

Thanks to all the makers and commissioners of the work described here. Thanks to Ben Hair for his painstaking gathering and compiling of the work, and to him and Marianna Filippou for the drawings, to Celia Knox for layout and drawing and to Dennis Gilbert for all his generous and fabulous images, to Maeve Bhavan for sitting in Hodges Place proofreading, and a special thanks to Prue Chiles for helping to find the words and for being positive, supportive and a wonderful editor.

Photographers
Dennis Gilbert (New Maltings, Hodges Place, Crowbrook, Brownstones, Holly Barn, front cover image)
Richard Haughton (College Road)
Charles Hosea (Rigg Beck)
Charles Ormerod (Rigg Beck)
Adelina Iliev (People Present and Past)
Fergus Knox (Four Tables, No Legs)
Simon Knox (Tudor House)

opposite ceramic bowls in bay window.

right bay window from garden.

above Bushey Hill Studio from gate.

opposite Bushey Hill Studio from garden.

overleaf sliding shutter and bay window.

pp 190–191 library.

KBA CARD ARCHIVE
LAIDLAW
DORMA GLASS
AUTOMATIC AND REVOLVING DOORS
Door Controls
@allgood
FSB @ allgood
HÄFELE
Furniture and Hardware Fittings
Architectural Ironmongery
Catalogue 2011
blum
Sealmaster
kerastar
JOHNSON-TILES
step
tretford
Bulletin Board
marmoleum
Woodland
Furniture Fittings and Applications
building proof
expamet

LEITZ
DLW LINOLEUM
Gerflor
Rolled Lead Sheet
RHEINZINK
TECU®-COPPER
FLAT ROOF SOLUTIONS
natural roofing slate
pure roofing
THE WHITE BOOK
HUDEVAD
PFC COROFIL - PASSIVE FIRE PROTECTION SYSTEMS
THE WHITE BOOK
The red book
Kingspan
STYROFOAM Solutions
Specialist Plaster
Technical Information Manual
BIDDENDEN COLLECTION
50x200mm WALL TILES
TOLLENS
CHROMO
PLANNING LAW
Law
THESAURUS
Green Building Handbook
Shadbolt veneers
Shadbolt
TIMBMET
ARCHITECTURE NOW!
BRE
LEITZ
DIGESTS 1997-2000
RIBA

Artifice books on architecture
10a Acton Street, London, WC1X 9NG
United Kingdom

+44 (0)20 7713 5097
sales@artificebooksonline.com
www.artificebooksonline.com

Design: Knox Bhavan with the assistance of Rachel Pfleger at Artifice books on architecture

British Library in Cataloguing Data
A CIP record for this book is available from the British Library

ISBN 978 1 908967 79 4

Artifice books on architecture, London, UK, is an environmentally responsible company. *craft material detail: Knox Bhavan* is printed on sustainably sourced paper.

reuse recycle reduce

Artifice
books on architecture